To Denis Stewart

with
cordial best wishes

Tom Stonier

22 - VIII - 90

Information and the Internal Structure of the Universe

An Exploration into Information Physics

Tom Stonier

Information and the Internal Structure of the Universe

An Exploration into Information Physics

Springer-Verlag
London Berlin Heidelberg New York
Paris Tokyo Hong Kong

Professor Tom Stonier, BA,MSc,PhD,FRSA
University of Bradford,
West Yorkshire, BD7 1DP, UK

ISBN 3-540-19599-8 Springer-Verlag Berlin Heidelberg New York
ISBN 0-387-19599-8 Springer-Verlag New York Berlin Heidelberg

Cover illustration: Starry sky (Vega), John Sanford, Science Photo Library; DNA double helix (B-form), Dr Arthur Lesk, Laboratory of Molecular Biology

British Library Cataloguing in Publication Data
Stonier, Tom, *1927–*
Information and the internal structure of the universe: an exploration into information physics.
1. Universe. Structure
I. Title
523.11
ISBN 3-540-19599-8

Library of Congress Cataloging-in-Publication Data
Stonier, Tom.
Information and the internal structure of the universe: an exploration into information physics/Tom Stonier.
p. cm.
ISBN 0-387-19599-8 (alk. paper)
1. Information theory. 2. Entropy (Information theory) 3. Physics.
4. Cosmology. I. Title.
Q360.S77 1990 90-9543
003'.54—dc20 CIP

Printed in Great Britain

Typeset by Saxon Printing Ltd., Saxon House, Derby
Printed and bound by The Alden Press, Osney Mead, Oxford
2128/3916-543210 Printed on acid-free, non-chlorine bleached paper

To my students whose
questions made me think
new thoughts

Acknowledgements

The author wishes to acknowledge with thanks the help he has received from students and colleagues all over the world in numerous free-ranging discussions. Particularly helpful have been discussions with Andrew Hopkins, Paul Quintas, Mark Seeger, Jefferson Stonier, and several of my professorial colleagues at Bradford University; Professors Stephen Barnett, Tony Johnson, Derry Jones, Vincent Walker, and John West. In addition, a detailed perusal of various drafts of the manuscript, followed by critical comments were provided by: Dr Philip Barker (Teesside), Dr Stafford Beer (Manchester), Dr Freeman Dyson (Princeton), Dr Brian Garvey (New Jersey), Dr Geoffrey Harrison (York), Dr Dilip Kondepudi (Winston-Salem), Dr Neil McEwan (Bradford), Dr Peter Monk (York), Dr James Noras (Bradford), Dr Brian Oakley (London), Dr Raymond Offen (London), and Dr Jiri Slechta (Leeds). Their input was crucial in preventing serious errors and in helping to present a complex and controversial theme in a more logical and presentable fashion. I wish in particular to express my gratitude to Neil McEwan for the discussions which led to quantifying the interconversion of energy and information.

With modern word-processing facilities, the temptation is to increase the number of manuscript drafts exponentially. I am afraid that the author succumbed to that temptation with great abandon – placing a terrible load not only on forests and the environment in general, but on the secretarial skills of Marlene Ellison in particular. I thank her for her forbearance and continued good cheer as well as her general competence and efficiency.

My wife Judith I wish to thank for maintaining the life support systems and providing joy to counter the gloom and darkness which periodically descend on most authors.

Finally Jamie Cameron and John Watson, in the best of editorial traditions, provided the kind of interest and support without which a book of this kind would never see the light of day. To them, as well as the rest of the Springer-Verlag (UK) team, in particular Linda Schofield and Jane Farrell, I am most grateful.

Tom Stonier
January 1990

Contents

Prologue

What is matter?
Never mind!
What is mind?
No matter!
(Albert Baez, 1967)

Matter and energy comprise the surface structure of the universe. The surface structure of the universe is readily perceivable to our senses.

The internal structure is more subtle. It is organised in a manner not so obvious: it consists not only of matter and energy, but of information as well.

Matter and energy is what we interface with physically. It is what we have come to recognise from earliest childhood on. It must also have been part of our instinctual heritage from the time of our earliest proto-human ancestors.

Matter is the ground we walk on, the rocks we throw, the objects we stub our toes or bang our heads on. Matter is what we manipulate with our hands.

Energy is what we perceive when we blink in the light or bask in the sun. Energy can cause us pain or frighten us, as when we burn our fingers, are tossed about in a ship, or are jolted by lightning.

Information is more subtle. It is true that it is also part of our daily experience. Every time we talk, read a newspaper, or watch television, we are busy absorbing or exchanging information. But we have always associated information with activities inside ourselves – inside our heads – not something that is "real" the way matter and energy are.

The purpose of this book is two-fold: First, to examine the proposition that "information" is as much a part of the physical universe as is matter and energy, and to consider the implications for the physical sciences of such a proposition. Second, to create a *foundation* on which to develop a general theory of information.

Actually, it is *not* the intention of the present work to develop a general theory of information. Instead, this book will explore the possibility of a new branch of physics – *information physics*. However, for reasons which should become self-evident – such an exploration constitutes a *necessary*, though not a *sufficient* condition for developing a science of information. Some of this material has already been published elsewhere (Stonier 1986a, 1986b, 1987). It is the intention of the author, that in a subsequent work, entitled *Beyond Chaos*, it will be possible to combine the insights from information physics with the insights from existing areas of knowledge such as cybernetics, semiotics, linguistics, syntactics, semantics, cognitive psychology, epistemology, etc, to create a synthesis from which will emerge the outline of a general theory of information. A third work, *Beyond Information*, will examine the evolution of intelligence from pre-biotic systems (ie, systems able to analyse their environment and respond in a manner so as to enhance their own survival), to post-human systems. An outline of this theme has been published elsewhere (Stonier 1988). The first step in any of these explorations, however, must be to establish and examine the physical basis of information.

The Author's Dilemma

One of the works which will be quoted from time to time is Erwin Schrödinger's classic little book *What is Life?* (1944). In his preface [p. vii] he states succinctly the dilemma the present author faces: "A scientist is supposed to have a complete and thorough knowledge, at first hand, of some subjects, and, therefore, is usually expected not to write on any topic of which he is not a master." Schrödinger, however, argues that "the spread, both in width and depth, of the multifarious branches of knowledge ... has confronted us with a queer dilemma.

We ... are only now beginning to acquire reliable material for welding together the sum-total of all that is known into a whole; but, on the other hand, it has become next to impossible for a single mind fully to command more than a small specialized portion of it." He concludes: "I can see no escape from this dilemma ... than that some of us should venture to embark on a synthesis of facts, and theories ... at the risk of making fools of ourselves."

Schrödinger also points out: "living matter, while not eluding the 'laws of physics' as established up to date, is likely to involve 'other laws of physics' hitherto unknown" [pp. 68–69]. In a sense, the present work may be considered as an extension of the dialogue between physicists and biologists begun by Schrödinger – this time, however, as seen from a biologist's point of view.

Literature Cited

AV Baez (1967) *The New College Physics*, WH Freeman, San Francisco.

E Schrödinger (1944) *What is Life?* Cambridge University Press.

T Stonier (1986a) Towards a new theory of information, *Telecom. Policy* 10(4):278–281.

T Stonier (1986b) What *is* information? *In Research and Development in Expert Systems III* (MA Bramer ed), pp. 217–230, Cambridge University Press.

T Stonier (1987) Towards a general theory of information – Information and entropy, *Future Computing Systems* 2(3), reprinted in *Aslib Proc.* 41(2):41–55 (1989).

T Stonier (1988) Machine intelligence and the long-term future of the human species, *AI & Society* 2:133–139.

· 1 ·

Information: Abstraction or Reality?

Introduction

Our perception of the world is the product of our historical experience. Historically, it was not until we had significant experience with time machines – mechanical clocks – that our concept of time developed. As Professor Whitrow (1975) has pointed out, most civilisations prior to post-seventeenth century Western civilisation, tended to regard time in a rather diffuse manner, and then as cyclic rather than linear [p. 11]. Clocks dissociated time from human event. Christian Huygens' invention of a successful pendulum clock in the middle of the seventeenth century provided the world with a device which could define time in terms of small, even and repetitious units. Furthermore, for all practical purposes grandfather's clock could go on ticking for ever. Thus Western culture became permeated with a sense of time passing, minute by minute, with time exhibiting the properties of homogeneity and continuity – a force in its own right [pp. 21–22].*

Similarly, it was not until we had significant experience with humanly created energy devices that energy began to be abstracted from the concept of matter. Before that, matter and energy were not distinct. An object might be hot or cold the way an object was hard or soft. These were properties of specific materials. Wool was warm, metal was cold. Wool was soft,

* More recently G. Szamosi (1986) has argued persuasively that the origin of the Western concept of time derived from medieval musicians, who in order to develop polyphony, needed to write down the temporal structures of the various melodies.

metal was hard. The fact that you could heat a metal could be explained by utilising the Aristotelian world view of the four elements – earth, water, air and fire. When you heated a metal, you were simply adding more fire to it.

The foundations of modern physics date back only about four centuries when Galileo studying the trajectories of cannonballs began to analyse force and motion. In like manner, it was only after about a century of experience with the steam engine, that the science of thermodynamics appeared. It was the experience with an energy engine which forced a much clearer definition of the concept "energy".

We are in a parallel historical situation today. Until recently we have had very little general experience with information machines. We have now had a new experience: computers – electronic devices capable of processing information – a process which previously could be accomplished only *inside* our heads. Increasingly, workers in the field of informatics – eg, software engineers, knowledge engineers, educators and trainers – have called for a better theoretical framework. For example, Gordon Scarrott (1986) has championed the need for a "science of information" which should investigate the "natural properties of information such as function, structure, dynamic behaviour and statistical features". Such an effort should "lead to a conceptual framework to guide systems design". Not only does the need of systems designers, software engineers, computer scientists, librarians and other specialists lead to an increasing preoccupation with the technology of information, but our outlook as a civilisation has been, and is continuing to be, affected by the advent of machine information processors and their derivative – artificial intelligence (see Stonier 1981, 1983, 1988).

There are two other strands in twentieth century experience which have given us a sense that information is more than something we manipulate inside our heads: First, there were the telephone engineers, who, like their colleagues on the telegraph and radio, were busy manipulating the transmission of information in a physical form (see review by Colin Cherry 1978) and secondly, the unequivocal demonstration that DNA carries the genetic information which determines how a single cell will develop into a sunflower, a mouse, or a man. In humans, the DNA carries the information which determines the sex, the colour of eyes, blood type and all the myriad of traits which provide each human being with the stamp of uniqueness. DNA, *a physical substance*, carries information, and has done so for more than a thousand million years. In contrast, it is doubtful whether the human brain has been around for much more than five million. Biological information systems, therefore, existed long before the evolution of the human (or any other) brain.

Can Information Exist Outside the Human Brain?

Information created or accumulated by human beings can be stored outside the human brain. Our civilisation has created whole institutions to store information outside our brains: libraries, art galleries, museums. Human information, that is information produced by human beings, may exist as patterns of energy or matter, whose *physical* reality is independent of human beings. Radio waves, computer disks and books are but three examples. Even if the radio waves diminish in intensity as they are dissipated in space to the point of vanishing, even if the information on computer disks may be compromised with time, and even if books mould or are somehow destroyed – for a time the information had a *physical* reality just as if it were a material product like an automobile. The fact that an automobile may rust out and end up as scrap does not deny its physical reality.

Information, unlike an automobile, is ethereal. This is why it may seem unreasonable to compare an information product such as a thought put down on paper, with a material product such as a car. However, the comparison is valid and may be made more explicit by considering another, humanly created, ethereal product – electricity supplied to the home. When we shut off the (electric) lights in our room, there is nothing left to show that a certain amount of electricity had been furnished to the house. Yet the electricity, supplied as a product from the generating station, had physical reality. Similarly, a thought spoken in that room, has disappeared as far as the physical expression of that thought – the sound waves – are concerned. However, both the electricity and the thought may be stored – for example, the former in a battery, the latter on a tape recording or in a book. We accept that a humanly created artefact such as an automobile, or humanly generated energy such as electricity in the home, both have physical reality. We must also recognise that humanly created information may exist in a physical form, as well.

We say a book contains information. We do not consider a book to be a human being. Therefore we must concede that information may exist apart from human beings. We may argue that a book, and the information contained therein, is of no use if it is not read by a human being. That is true. But that does not negate the fact that the information is there, on tap, as it were. The matter is similar to the old question: "If a tree falls, and no one is there to hear it, does it produce sound?" The answer is *no* if one insists that sound exists only if it causes vibrations in a human eardrum. The answer is *yes* if one defines sound as patterns of compressed air produced by the crashing tree.

The former interpretation is egocentric and obstructs any intelligent analysis of the world outside. To be consistent, the modern equivalent of the "human ear drum" interpretation would imply that if we leave the lights on in a room, as soon as we leave the room, the light no longer shines. Or as soon as we shut off our radio, the room is no longer filled with radio waves.

The radio illustrates an important point. The electromagnetic radiation comprising the radio waves carries a lot of information. However, we cannot perceive that information until we have a *detector* – a radio, and then, and only then, can our eardrums detect the information.

Can Information Be Processed Outside the Human Brain?

Computers, like books and gramophone records, can store information. However, they can also process information. The information which comes out of a computer may be entirely different from what went in. At the most primitive level of computation, the human operator puts in two numbers, let us say "2" and "3", plus the instruction to add them. The computer will process this information and come out with "5", a symbol not entered by the human operator. In this age of the pocket calculator, we are no longer impressed by such a feat. Not even when the calculator, in a twinkling, gives us the square root of 14,379. "It is merely following a program" is our platitudinal explanation. What is overlooked in our anthropocentric eagerness to avoid the possibility that computers engage in a rudimentary form of thinking, is that the information which went into the computer is different from what came out. The computer engaged in information processing. This is very different from a book or a gramophone which merely regurgitates the information which went in.

Computers are able to carry out logical, as well as mathematical and algebraic, operations. Sophisticated ("intelligent") data bases can provide answers based on a combination of data and logic. For example, the personnel data base of a large company may respond to the question "Who is Frank Jones' boss?" with the answer "John Smith", even though that specific piece of information was never entered into the computer. What had been entered was the name and position of every employee including which department they worked in. That involved mere data storage. But the computer was also given certain logical instructions on how to operate on this data base. For example, the instruction: "The head of a department is the boss of any employee working within that department" would allow it, using logical operations, to deduce that John Smith headed up the operation of which Frank Jones was a part. A young child accomplishing such a feat would be considered very clever.

Forms of Human Information and its Communication

Just as there exist different forms of energy – mechanical, chemical, electrical, heat, sound, light, nuclear, etc – so do there exist different forms of information. Human information represents only one form of information. We will discuss non-human forms later. However, human information itself, may be stored and communicated in a wide variety of ways and represent many different forms.

The systems for storing and processing information contained within the human brain are so complex and so mysterious as to constitute the last great frontier of the biological sciences. When compared to a computer, the human brain exhibits substantially greater complexity in at least three areas (as reviewed by Stonier 1984). First, the circuitry is incredibly more complex: Not only does the brain contain of the order of 10^{11} cells, but a single brain cell may be connected to thousands of other cells. Each neuron, in turn, may prove to be equivalent to a transputer rather than a transistor. Second, the transmission system is different. In a computer one is dealing with electrons moving along a conductor. Nerve impulses, in contrast, involve the progressive depolarisation of membranes. This device allows the transmission system to be regulated much more delicately and relates to the third major difference: Information handling in the present generation of computers is digital. In the human nervous system there exist dozens of neurotransmitters and other related substances which can enhance or inhibit nerve impulses – the whole system is a finely tuned and integrated network of analogue devices.

The nature of the information inside people's heads must be different from that contained inside a computer. In addition, the form information takes as it is being communicated between two people, two computers, or between people and computers, must differ again. Just as there exist many forms of information, so there exist many *means* by which information may be transmitted, or transduced (converted from one form to another).

Consider the information on this page. It is being transmitted to the reader's eye by light. The light striking the retina is converted to nerve impulses which are propagated by the sequential depolarisation of membranes. At the synapses between the nerve cells of the brain, the information is converted to pulses of chemical neurotransmitters which, in turn, trigger further neurological activities, branching in many directions. Ultimately, these events lead to a host of brain activities: short-term memory storage, comparison with existing information at many levels (from comparing pictures of the printed letters and words, and their meanings, to comparing the concepts of this article with the reader's view of the world), long-term memory storage and the myriad of other, still mysterious, thought processes associated with assimilating and analysing new information.

At some point in the future, the reader may convert the patterns of neural information stored in the brain into sound waves via nerve impulses to the vocal chords. Sound waves, represent a mechanical coding of information. The sound waves impinge upon the ears of the listener where the information is now converted from pulses of mechanical energy into nerve impulses by the motion of microscopic hair-like organelles in the inner ear. These nerve impulses enter the brain of the listener where the information will undergo a processing similar to that originally taking place in the brain of the reader.

Alternatively, the reader might speak into a telephone where the information is transduced from patterns of compressed air molecules travelling at the speed of sound into electronic pulses travelling down a copper wire closer to the speed of light. These electronic pulses travelling down a wire, might, in turn be converted into pulses of light travelling down an optical fibre. Or the reader might speak into a microphone either for broadcast, in which case the information is transduced into patterns of electromagnetic waves traversing the airwaves, or into a tape recorder where the electronic pulses are converted into magnetic pulses, then "frozen" into the tape by having atoms, responding to magnetism, arrange themselves physically into patterns of information within the tape.

The above represents one set of cycles which illustrate the communication of human information. Note what it entailed: the information was propagated as:

1. Patterns of light (from the book to the eye).
2. Pulses of membrane depolarisation (from the eye to the brain).
3. Pulses of chemical substances (between individual nerves).
4. Pulses of compressed air molecules, ie sound waves (emitted by the larynx of the speaker).
5. Pulses of mechanical distortion in liquid or solid (inside the ear or the telephone mouthpiece).
6. Pulses of electrons in a telephone wire.
7. Pulses of light in optical fibres.
8. Pulses of radio waves.
9. Pulses of magnetism (inside the earpiece of a telephone or the speaker of a radio).

The information was stored as printing in a book, in the human brain, and on magnetic tape. The first involved patterns of dye molecules; the second, probably patterns of neural connections; and the last, patterns of magnetised regions. It was converted from one form into another in the retina of the eye, at the synapsis between nerve cells, in the larynx, in the inner ear, in the telephone, the radio transmitter, the radio receiver, and the tape recorder.

The reader might also have decided to store the information on a computer, or in a file by photoduplicating it, or by typing it out, thereby committing the information once more to patterns of dye molecules superimposed on paper molecules. From cave wall paintings and carvings on wood or stone, to bubble memories and satellite communication, human information is capable of being stored, transmitted or transduced in a very large number of ways – and the number continues to increase.

It is important to note that the means of propagating information, as exemplified by the above list of nine, usually involved *pulses* of waves (light, sound, radio waves), *pulses* of electrons, or *pulses* affecting matter or its organisation. The fact that information may be divided up into small, discrete packets is utilised by communications engineers for packet switching to allow several users to use the same facility simultaneously. The idea that information is an independent entity, comes naturally to the communications engineer since the pioneering work of Hartley, Shannon and others. Thus in a standard text such as D.A. Bell's *Information Theory and its Engineering Application* (1968) one finds stated clearly on p. 1: "Information ... is a measurable quantity which is independent of the physical medium by which it is conveyed." This does not necessarily mean that it has a *physical* reality. Bell compares information to the more abstract term "pattern". However, it does imply an existence of its own.

Although the communications engineers treat information as an abstract quantity, they do not follow this idea to its logical conclusion – viz, information *exists*. Perhaps part of the problem of recognising and accepting the idea that information has physical reality and constitutes an intrinsic property of the universe, stems from the fact that we ourselves are so deeply embedded in the processing and transmitting of it.

Biological Information Systems

One of the great advances in the biological sciences over the past few decades has been the decoding of DNA (deoxyribonucleic acid). That is, not only has it been possible to establish beyond a reasonable doubt that DNA can carry the information which is transmitted from one generation to the next, it has been possible to decode the manner in which these messages are being communicated. Among other interesting findings, biological scientists uncovered the fact that the messages transmitted by this information system are apparently understood by all forms of extant life on this planet – bacteria and sunflowers, mice and men. The amount and the nature of the information contained in the DNA may vary from one organism to the next, but the method of coding it into a DNA molecule is the same.

The fact that the same piece of DNA produces similar consequences in different organisms provides the basic information on which that newest of knowledge industries, the genetic engineering industry, is developing. It is also of great theoretical interest to scientists studying cancer and other biological phenomena (for example, certain parasitic bacteria have been shown to transfer a large piece of DNA to the cells of host plants, conferring new genetic information on the cells and thereby causing them to become cancerous).

As it has become apparent that the structure of DNA contains information which can be transmitted, so has it become apparent that other macromolecules and cellular structures such as RNA (ribonucleic acid), structural proteins, and membranes also possess transmissible information. That is, these substances either can be replicated in the cell (thereby transferring the information to the next generation of molecules), or may be important in their own growth by acting as templates which mould the future, organised arrangement of atoms and molecules.

The non-random distribution of atoms and molecules in living systems, that is, *the intricate organisation of matter and energy which makes possible that phenomenon which we call life, is itself a product of the vast store of information contained within the system itself.*

Inorganic Information Systems

Is it possible to apply these considerations to simpler, non-living forms of organisation? Let us consider the growth of crystals. The entire chip industry is based on the insight that it is possible to obtain a highly purified form of silicon by letting crystals of silicon "grow" in the appropriate solutions. Even more dramatic is the "growth" of an inorganic crystal in the autocatalytic reaction when a small crystal of manganese dioxide (MnO_2), dropped into a solution of potassium permanganate ($KMnO_4$), causes the latter to be converted into the former. The organisation, ie, the spatial arrangement of the atoms in such a crystal, acts as a template for other atoms being added on, causing molecules moving at random in a liquid to be bound into a non-random arrangement – thereby bringing order out of chaos (see Prigogine and Stengers 1985).

In recent years a whole new line of investigations has centred on the possibility that the origin of life initially involved clay minerals (for a comprehensive review see Cairns-Smith and Hartman 1986). Clay minerals are aperiodic crystals whose essentially crystalline character provides an underlying regularity. As the editors point out [p. 23], this regularity "is invariably modulated by irregularities that could in principle hold information". Alan Mackay, one of the contributors to the above volume, describes a crystal matrix as having the characteristic of an abacus on which it is possible to write an arbitrary message. Mackay also defines a "naked gene" [p. 142] as a system in which: "A message is simply reproduced." A naked gene, originally, need not relate to anything. A.G. Cairns-Smith goes on to describe a class of objects which may be considered as "proper crystal genes" [pp. 142–152]. First, a proper crystal gene should self-assemble in an orderly way as normal crystals do. If the template were horizontal, and the growing crystal kept building up a vertical stack of the same pattern, then fracturing it along a horizontal plane would result in two pieces such that the bottom piece could continue building the pattern from the bottom up (as before), while the top could build the same pattern from the top down. Actually, the two surfaces, top and bottom, would not look identical but would be enantiomeric. In such a system, the information being replicated would be in two dimensions. The information carrier, however, would have a robust, three-dimensional structure, with the information contained within it highly redundant. Any stable irregularity would be efficiently transmitted from one generation of crystalline structures to the next as long as sideways growth did not occur, and as long as cleavages occurred exclusively in a plane perpendicular to the direction of growth. Cairns-Smith goes on to consider other systems which would work and concludes that there are four "critical and general requirements" [p. 147]:

(1) *disorder*, to provide information capacity; (2) *order*, for replicative fidelity; (3) *growth*, so as to duplicate the information, and (4) *cleavage*, so as to complete the replication process.

Of these four general requirements, one must be cautious about interpreting the first: *Disorder* does *not* provide information! Mackay's naked gene needs no disorder to exist and multiply. Disorder could, in fact, destroy it! As will be discussed in the next chapter, information is a function of *organisation*; disordering a system causes it to *lose* information. However, disorder can provide the mechanism for altering the structure of a system so as to allow a "mutation" to appear. If there existed no possibilities for introducing variations, then there would be no possibility for the system to evolve. Cairns-Smith's first requirement, therefore, might better be restated as: "*disorder*, to provide *mutations*": That is, the term "information capacity", derived from the communications engineers, should be replaced by the more relevant term "mutation", used by biologists.

The presence of a gene clay crystal (which breeds true to form) in a complex environment made up of a mixture of other inorganic, and organic substances, could influence the organisation of that environment. For example, it could affect the circumstances under which various compounds precipitate out of a solution, or alternatively, affect the growth and composition of other clays. Insofar as organic molecules can influence the rates of crystal growth of clays, just as clays can bind organic compounds, one can create endless complexities which, however, in principle, might be strongly influenced – perhaps even regulated – by sets of crystal genes. We would be looking at a primitive genotype/phenotype system.

The questions explored by the various authors in Cairns-Smith and Hartman (1986), touched on above, are worthy of deeper considerations and will be dealt with in a future work (*Beyond Information*).

Non-human Information Processing

The discovery that DNA, which may be isolated in a test tube as a crystal, contains the information necessary for reproducing a virus, or a baby, represents the sort of historical experience which allowed us to differentiate between human and non-human information. However, the story does not end there. It is not only that "information" has existed for a billion years prior to the advent of the human species – for a billion years that information has been *processed*. DNA, by itself is useless unless the *information* is processed by a cell. A crystal of DNA in a test tube is like a book on a shelf: If left unread, its information cannot become useful. Likewise with DNA: In order for its information to fulfil its biological function, it requires the complex machinery of a living cell to decode and process it. Thus, not only is information not a uniquely human attribute, but *information processing* is not either. Biological systems have been processing information since their origin. One could, in fact, interpret the entire evolutionary history of living systems in terms of their ability to create ever more efficient means of preserving and processing relevant information. It was this evolution of information systems which led to ever more complex, differentiated forms of organisation.

Again, as in the previous discussion, there is no reason to limit the above considerations to organic systems only. A crystal of silicon acting as a template may be said to be processing the information in its environment as it grows. It is true that this form of information processing is much more primitive than that which occurs in a cell. Growth of a crystal is by "accretion"; that is, atoms of silicon are simply added on externally. In contrast, growth of a nucleic acid is metabolic and interstitial: The cell absorbs foreign matter which is processed into complex sub-units such as purines or pyrimidines, and ribose or desoxyribose sugars. These are combined with phosphoric acid units to create nucleotides which are assembled into nucleic acids by further processing. All this involves an incredibly complex but highly integrated set of enzymes and other components which make up the metabolic machinery of the cell. To compare the growth of a crystal with the replication of a DNA molecule is like comparing the information processing carried out by first-generation electronic computers such as ENIAC, with that of advanced neural network computers. Nevertheless, if varying in degrees of complexity, all of the above systems are capable of engaging in information processing.

Some Epistemological Considerations

The major concern of the present book is with information and the structure of the physical universe. *Information* as used in this book, is a property of the universe – it is a part of its "internal" structure.

In contrast to physical information, there exists human information which includes the information created, interpreted, organised or transmitted by human beings. Actually, the term "information" as traditionally used, has been defined in a number of different, sometimes contradictory, ways. For a helpful review by an information practitioner, the reader is referred to M. Broadbent (1984).

The term "information" includes "data" on the one hand, and "knowledge", "insight" and "wisdom", on the other. A datum is a small chunk of information. Usually the term information is thought of as organised data, or "facts" organised into a coherent pattern. However, the demarcation has always been fuzzy and is avoided here by considering human information as comprising a spectrum, with a single bit in a binary system as the smallest unit of information, while knowledge, insight and wisdom would comprise the other end, exhibiting increasing levels of complexity. Patterns of information, at whatever level of complexity, need sensors to be perceived, and "intelligence" to be analysed and processed. It is processing information into new patterns that the human brain is so good at. Knowledge, insight and wisdom represent the increasing complexity of organised information in people's heads.

Human knowledge, therefore, may be defined as organised information in people's heads, or in (human) information storage and retrieval systems such as books, computer programs, audio tapes, medieval stained glass windows, etc. Human knowledge is the way human beings organise information into patterns comprehensible to human beings. In this sense, knowledge represents the intellectual constructs of human beings organising human information.

Note that in all this we side-step the epistemological question of what is knowable. We define human *information* as that which is perceived, created, or transmitted, without making a judgement as to its accuracy or reliability. Similarly, human *knowledge* is defined as organised information, implying that it is information which has been processed, without judging in the present analysis, the merits or validity of the process.

If *information* has an independent reality, *meaning* does not. Meaning involves the interpretation of information in relation to some *context*. Such a process requires an information processor (a human being or some other system) which relates the information to some context. That is, the information stored in a book does not become meaningful until it is read and understood. The same may be said of a radio broadcast, which in order to become meaningful must first be detected by tuning a radio to the right frequency. However, that process in itself is not a sufficient condition. A radio picking up morse code signals or a foreign language broadcast would provide information in a detectable, but not necessarily comprehensible, form. The same may be said of a book written in a foreign language, incomprehensible to the reader.

Thus *we must not confuse the detection and/or interpretation of information with information itself*. Patterns of electromagnetic radiation in the room, or the print on the page contain information irrespective of whether we turn on our radio or open the book. This is true even if the broadcast originated from outer space and involved a non-human language, or the book was written in a "dead" language no longer understood by any living human being.

In the present work, and this is crucial to the entire analysis, *information is considered to be distinct from the system which interprets, or in some other way processes, such information*. If a molecule of DNA contains information, the expression of that information will not materialise until it has been processed by a cell. There is a distinction however between the coding on the DNA molecule, and the cell which interprets or processes that coding. The former (the code), represents pure information, the latter, the processor of that information. Similarly, a book contains information, the reader represents the processor.

Literature Cited

DA Bell (1968) *Information Theory and its Engineering Application*, 4th edn, Sir Isaac Pitman & Sons, London.

M Broadbent (1984) Information management and educational pluralism, *Education for Information* 2:209–227.

AG Cairns-Smith and H Hartman (1986) *Clay Minerals and the Origin of Life*, Cambridge University Press.

C Cherry (1978) *On Human Communication*, 3rd edn, The MIT Press, Cambridge, Mass.

AL Mackay (1986) The crystal abacus, in *Clay Minerals and the Origin of Life* (AG Cairns-Smith and H Hartman ed), pp. 140–143, Cambridge University Press.

I Prigogine and I Stengers (1985) *Order out of Chaos*, Flamingo/Fontana, London.

G Scarrott (1986) The need for a "science" of information, *J. Inform. Technol.* 1(2):33–38.

T Stonier (1981) The natural history of humanity : past, present and future, *Int. J. Man–Machine Stud.* 14:91–122.

T Stonier (1983) *The Wealth of Information : A Profile of the Post-Industrial Society*, Thames/Methuen, London.

T Stonier (1984) Computer psychology, *Educational and Child Psychol.* 1(2 & 3):16–27.

T Stonier (1986a) Towards a new theory of information, *Telecom. Policy* 10(4):278–281.

T Stonier (1986b) What is information? in *Research and Development in Expert Systems III* (MA Bramer ed), pp. 217–230, Cambridge University Press.

T Stonier (1987) Towards a general theory of information – Information and entropy, *Future Computing Systems* 2(3), Reprinted in *Aslib Proc.* 41(2):41–55 (1989).

T Stonier (1988) Machine intelligence and the long-term future of the human species, *AI & Society* 2:133–139.

G Szamosi (1986) *The Twin Dimensions: Inventing Time and Space*, McGraw-Hill, New York.

GJ Whitrow (1975) *The Nature of Time*, Penguin Books.

· 2 ·

Information Physics: An Introduction

The Reality of Information

To reiterate : *Information exists.* It does not need to be *perceived* to exist. It does not need to be *understood* to exist. It requires no intelligence to interpret it. It does not have to have *meaning* to exist. It exists.

Without this insight it becomes impossible either to understand the physical universe, or to try to develop a general theory of information. And without a general theory, it not only becomes impossible to convert knowledge engineering and software production into a science, it becomes impossible to truly understand the behaviour of advanced systems – biological, social and economic.

To review the argument. A book contains information whether it is read or not. The information is there even if it is not transferred to a human reader. Even if the book is written in Finnish, a language about as incomprehensible to an English reader as possible, the book still contains information.

An English reader attempting to decipher a book written in Finnish, provides us with a paradigm for understanding the dichotomy between information and meaning. In fact, an analysis of "books" in general, allows us to understand that the relationship between *information* and *meaning* involves a spectrum. That is why there is so much confusion: The phenomenon we call "meaning" involves a gradient of relationships between physical information and mental interpretations.

At one extreme is a book written in a language which is native to us, and pitched at a level appropriate to our understanding of the subject under discussion. Such a book not only *contains* a lot of information, it also *conveys* a lot of information. The book is able to convey a lot of information because the information has *meaning* for us. The reason the information has meaning for us is that we are able to put the information conveyed into a personal *context*. Such a context consists of knowledge structures inside our brain which may act as an *information environment* for a specific piece of new information. The richer this internal information environment, the greater the context into which the new information may be placed, and the more meaningful it becomes. That is, the information conveyed by a book is a function of the intellectual information environment present as knowledge structures already existing inside the reader's brain.*

To return to the spectrum : Next is a book written in our native language but about a subject unfamiliar to us. Unfamiliar terms and concepts make it more difficult to understand. The same is true for a child reading material beyond its reading age. This type of decline in the amount of information conveyed to a reader is epitomised by comparing "highbrow" newspapers with tabloids. The former pitch their vocabulary and style to an audience with about a 16-year-old reading age. The latter pitch it at a 12-year-old one. Adults whose educational background precludes them from fully understanding *The Times* have no trouble reading a tabloid. This does not mean that *The Times* contains less information.

Next, down the ladder of meaning are books written in a foreign language. For a person speaking only English, western European languages may have some words which are readily recognisable. But phrases and sentences have no meaning. For the English reader, books written in a non-Indo-European language such as Finnish, virtually no words are meaningful. However, the letters are familiar and the book still has meaning for the reader at two levels: The reader recognises the book as a book, and the reader recognises the letters. The *letters* still have meaning for the reader.

---

* These matters will be discussed in greater detail in subsequent works: *Beyond Chaos* and *Beyond Information*.

Not so if the book has been translated into Arabic. Now the reader can discern no meaning in the letters. The text conveys *almost* no information to the reader, yet the linguistic information *contained* by the book is virtually the same as in the English original.

The reader, familiar with books will still recognise two things, however: First, that the book *is* a book. Second, that the squiggles on the page represent a pattern of abstractions which probably makes sense to someone who understands the meaning of those squiggles. Therefore, the book as such, will still have some meaning for the English reader, even if the *content* of the text has none.

Let us go to a more extreme case. Not a book, but a stone, or a rock with engravings in an ancient language no longer understood by anyone alive. Does such a stone not *contain* human information even if it is not decipherable? Suppose at some point in the future, basic knowledge about linguistics and clever computer aids allow us to decipher it? Or suppose someone discovers the equivalent of a Rosetta stone which allows us to translate it into a known language, and then into English? Can one really say that the stone contained no information prior to translation?

It is possible to argue that the stone, prior to deciphering contained only *latent* information. That is, information is not truly information until it has been read, or in some other fashion acquired by a human being. The act of absorbing information is what makes it into *real* information.

This appears to be the *common-sense* understanding of the term "information" (as ascertained by the author in numerous discussions with colleagues and others).

The undecipherable hieroglyphics on our hypothetical stone, present a dilemma to this common-sense interpretation of the term information. Because of our historical experience with dead languages which have been deciphered, we recognise intuitively that the stone contains information. But what if no-one ever deciphers it? At this point one could take one of three positions:

1. Even though the stone has "writing" on it, it contains *no* information because it makes no sense to anybody.
2. The stone contains a sort of information, which however does not constitute real information until somebody *can* read it.

3. The stone *does* contain information even though its text *conveys* no information.

These three positions are mutually exclusive. If the reader of this treatise holds to the first position, he or she is not going to accept any of the subsequent discussion. Those holding to the second position will need to make a shift: What they consider to be "real" information will be referred to in the present work as "meaningful" information, ie, the information which can be conveyed to a receptor. What they might consider as "latent" or "potential" information will be considered as real information – as real as the *energy* contained by an object or a system which is not being observed, or which is not being made to perform work. That is, the heat contained by such a system exists whether we observe it or not. When we do measure it, we measure it in terms of the energy contained by the system. The same holds true for information.

Let us continue the spectrum : We assumed that the markings on the stone were hieroglyphics. What if they were mere decorative patterns with no explicit message? Or how about finding a paleolithic bone with regular markings on it? Are those marks merely decorations, or are they tallies of some sort, or a calendar? The stone or the bone has less meaning for us still. Nevertheless, it does still contain information, specifically *human* information – assuming that we can establish that the patterns were the product of human activity. (In addition, the stone and the bone contain non-human information insofar as they exhibit patterns of organisation.)

The idea that communicated human information may have a physical reality of its own, apart from its human origin, may be illustrated by considering the possible fate of a radio message beamed out into space: Moving at the speed of light, it cannot be recovered. The message comprises a pattern superimposed on a carrier. However, it is now divorced from its Earthling originators. All human life on earth may be extinguished by a nuclear disaster or by an interstellar catastrophe. The pattern continues to be propagated. Theoretically, it is possible that the pattern is deciphered by other intelligences. But even if it is not, the message continues moving through space – a physical entity oblivious of what may or may not be happening to its creators on earth.

It becomes *impossible* to develop a general theory of information as long as we confuse the various aspects of information with its transfer, processing, or interpretation. This book assumes that there exists a dichotomy between (1) the information intrinsically *contained* by a system, and (2) the information which may be *conveyed* by the system to some receptor!

A classic literary illustration of this dichotomy is represented by Conan Doyle's Sherlock Holmes and Dr Watson. Items which conveyed no information of special interest to Watson, represented vital clues for Holmes. The actual information *contained* by the item was the same; what it *conveyed*, however, depended on whether the receptor was a Sherlock Holmes, or a Dr Watson.

The Heart of the Concept

It has now been demonstrated beyond a reasonable doubt that DNA molecules contain, and are able to transmit, large amounts of information (sufficient to program a single cell so that it can grow into a human being). Similarly, crystals of manganese dioxide or of silicon contain sufficient information to create more of themselves, and crystals of clay exhibit patterns of organisation which, like an abacus, can carry information. Furthermore, we observe that these biological, proto-biological, and mineral systems not only contain information, but exhibit information processing capabilities as well.

The information which is processed by the solution of potassium permanganate interacting with a crystal of manganese dioxide – or by the human cell interacting with a strand of DNA – is the organisational pattern of the carrier of information, the MnO_2 or the DNA. That is, in each and every instance, the information is physically encoded as patterns of organisation. This association leads to the first axiom of information physics:

Information and organisation are intimately interrelated.

From this axiom we derive the following theorems:

1. **All organised structures contain information,** and as a corollary: **No organised structure can exist without containing some form of information.**

2. **The addition of information to a system manifests itself by causing a system to become more organised, or reorganised.**
3. **An organised system has the capacity to release or convey information.**

Let us examine the above theorems, beginning with the first: Any physical system which exhibits organisation contains information. Information organises space and time. The definition of the term "information" becomes analogous to the physicist's definition of the term "energy": *Energy* is defined as the capacity to perform work. *Information* is defined as the capacity to organise a system – or to maintain it in an organised state. As we shall discuss later, it becomes impossible to perform "useful" work without an input of *both* energy and information. Conversely, all work brings about a change in organisation, hence information.

Organization is a reflection of order. A structure or system may be said to be organised if it exhibits order. *Order* is a non-random arrangement of the parts of the structure or system. *Randomness* is the opposite of order, keeping in mind that certain forms of apparent randomness exhibit significant order, eg, a perfectly uniform distribution. For this reason, the terms *chaos* and *disorder* are preferable. Any quantitative analysis of information must be based, at least in part, on measuring either the order, or the chaos of a system.

Analysing the information content of a chaotic system is made more problematical by the fact that a system may only *appear* to be chaotic: That is, such a system actually is responding to a simple algorithm – the apparent unpredictability reflects the fact that trivial variations in initial conditions may have a major impact on the system's final behaviour (Gleick 1988).

Organisation and information are, by definition, closely interlinked. However, they are different: One cannot have a shadow without light, but a shadow and light are not the same thing. A shadow is the manifestation of light interacting with an opaque object. Likewise, organisation is the manifestation of information interacting with matter and energy.

It is important to emphasise the conceptual necessity for an abstract term such as "information". Information is a quantity which may be altered from one form to another. Information is a quantity which may be transferred from one system to another. This is not true, at least to the same degree, for the more concrete terms "order", "organisation", "pattern", or "structure". The matter parallels the difference between the terms "energy" and "heat". Energy is capable of being transformed from one form to another, as well as being transferred from one system to another. In contrast, the limitations of the less abstract concept "heat" (a quantity directly perceptible to our physical senses), cannot explain how heating a boiler causes a locomotive to move, or a light bulb to light up in response to the electricity generated by a steam turbine.

Likewise, "information" may be transformed from one form to another, as for example, when dictating a manuscript: Patterns of sound waves end up transcribed as words on a printed page. It is easy to understand that the information was transferred and transformed via the stenographer and printer, from the spoken to the written word. It is not clear how the oscillating molecules of air comprising the sound pattern end up as apparently unrelated patterns of dye molecules on a printed page. The matter becomes even more mysterious when one eliminates the human intermediaries and speaks into a voice-to-print device. The structure of the phonemes making up a word is not the same as the structure of the printed syllables making up the same word. The information content, however, may be the same for both.

Information, like energy, is an abstract quantity. Communications engineers have recognised since Hartley's time, over half a century ago, that information may be treated as an abstract quantity. What the present work proposes is more than that, viz, that information, like energy, also possesses a *physical* reality.

To be more precise, *heat* (involving uncorrelated phonons in a crystal or randomly moving molecules in a gas) is the product of the interaction between matter and pure energy. *Structure* is the product of the interaction between matter and pure information. Energy, in pre-relativity physics, was considered as the more abstract quantity which, when added to matter, manifested itself as heat. Likewise, information may be considered as the more abstract quantity which, when added to matter, manifests itself as structure (organisation).

As will be discussed in a later chapter, such a conceptualisation of information leads to a different quantitative definition from that of the communications engineers. Such a definition also differs from the standard dictionary definition which defines *information* as, for example: knowledge, news, or what is told. Dictionaries go on to define *knowledge* as all that is, or may be known. Knowing is defined as: recognising, perceiving with certainty, being aware (of), being acquainted with. There are other, more specialised meanings provided by dictionaries, but the gist is that information is either a form of knowledge, or equivalent to it. Dictionaries define knowledge and information purely in implicitly human terms. This is in marked contrast to the principle that information is a property of the universe – that it comprises the "internal" structure of the universe.

Human information may involve the *perception* of that "internal" structure. Every time scientists define a constant such as the gas constant, Avogadro's number, Boltzmann's or Planck's constant, etc, they have discovered another aspect of the organisation of the universe. Each such discovery represents the human perception of the information contained within physical systems.

Aspects of *human* information systems, including the terms knowledge, meaning, significance, intelligence, etc will be explored in a future work, *Beyond Chaos*. The present work is concerned with the physics of information systems – systems whose reality is independent of human perception and which therefore transcends it.

To sum up: All regular patterns contain information. The mathematics of chaos has demonstrated that even apparently highly irregular patterns, may be the product of some rather simple algorithm which underlies the chaos. To the argument that what we are really talking about is "patterns" and "organisation", the answer is that "information" is a more abstract generalisation which, in the long run, one needs in order to measure it by some universal measure such as "bits". It becomes as difficult to measure quantitatively a pattern or a structure in terms of bits without the aid of the abstract concept "information", as it is to measure in joules the output of light by a lamp without the more abstract concept "energy".

Information: The Hidden Dimension

Information is an implicit component of virtually every single equation governing the laws of physics. Since Galileo's classic experiments, physicists and engineers have described all motion in terms of distance and time. All motion involves a reorganisation of the universe – as such, all motion may be considered to represent an "information act".

Information is found in any analysis which involves vectors. The term "direction" is an information term. It implies a relationship to existing axes (real or imagined). Obviously "direction" is neither a form of matter nor of energy. Similarly, changes in distance and time measure the changes in the "information status" of the system containing the moving body. Specifically, they measure the body in relation to its environment. In fact, in order to measure distance and time properly, one requires some organised frame of reference – real or imagined. The description of motion, therefore, involves a statement about the changes in the information status of the system.

When analysing the motion of a body one needs to distinguish between three separate (though interrelated) phenomena: (1) The *force* applied to the body which causes it to move (or change its motion) in the first place, (2) the *momentum* of the body in motion, and (3) the *motion* itself. Force and momentum represent aspects of pure energy, although by definition, both contain the dimensions of time and distance. However, the motion itself, ie, the trajectory of the particle, is pure information, describing the reorganisation of the system as the particle moves from locus A to locus B in some frame of reference.

If "motion", as distinct from its cause or effect, comprises a form of information, that does not preclude a moving particle from, at the same time, possessing energy. If such a moving particle has mass, then its energy can be measured in terms of its momentum. Even if it lacks mass, as in the case of a photon, using the relativity equation it may be shown to possess momentum *providing* it moves with velocity c – the speed of light. (There exists also the theoretical possibility of moving particles lacking both mass and momentum – ie, particles possessing only information – a matter to be speculated on in Appendix A.)

All constants reflect some organisational property of the system described. Without such an organisational property, the fixed relationship defining any given constant could not exist. Therefore, whether one considers Avogadro's number, Heisenberg's or Boltzmann's constants, or the speed of light –

all define some fixed relationship or sets of relationships, within the system. Such fixed relationships imply order within the system, which, of course, reflects the information contained by the system.

In a similar vein, Pauli's exclusion principle, so vital to the organisation of matter, must reflect an information property of atomic shells. Fundamental particles themselves, may exhibit information properties: Quarks are assigned properties such as charm or beauty. Likewise, up and down imply some relational property characteristic of systems containing information. The same may be said of electric charge. For although the separation of opposite charges (or the forcing together of like charges) may set up a force, a single charge by itself represents an information property of the particle carrying the charge.

Distance measures the space between two objects or imaginary points. Time measures the interval between two events. Both distance and time represent forms of information. However, these two forms of information are as different from each other as, for example, are electromagnetic radiation and mechanical energy. Having said that, time and distance are interconvertible in relativistic terms just as the mechanical energy driving an electricity generating turbine may end up as light emitted by an electric bulb. Thus not only are various forms of energy interconvertible, in like manner, so are various forms of information. Furthermore, energy and information are also readily interconvertible between each other – a matter to be examined later in conjunction with entropy, work, and potential energy.

If distance d, time t, and direction, are forms of information, then "velocity" – the rate of change of a moving body's position in a particular direction with time – must be a form of information; and if velocity represents information, then "acceleration" (velocity per unit of time) must also be a form of information. This raises the question whether the classical equation relating force F to mass m times acceleration a, ie

$$F = ma$$

implies that one may consider force to be the mathematical product of mass and information, and likewise, that the equation for work W:

$$W = Fd$$

implies that work, too, is a mathematical product of mass and information. (The same argument would hold for non-uniform velocities v:

$$v = \mathrm{d}r/\mathrm{d}t$$

where r, the positional vector, also represents a form of information.)

Literature Cited

J Gleick (1988) *Chaos*, Penguin Books, New York.

· 3 ·

Information and Entropy: The Mathematical Relationship

Information and Organisation

As stated repeatedly, if a system exhibits organsation, it contains information. Since organisation reflects the ordered arrangement of the constituent parts of a system, and since order is in opposition to disorder, it stands to reason that information and disorder are inversely related: The more disordered the system, the less is its information content.

Related to the concept of disorderliness is the thermodynamic concept of probability. In traditional thermodynamic systems, in general, the closer to equilibrium, the more disordered a system, the more probable the state. Thus on one side, the properties of disorderliness, probability, and lack of information tend to go hand in hand, while on the other, organisation, improbability and information correlate.

Thermodynamic probability relates to entropy and the previous sentence implies that a highly disordered, high probability state is associated with high entropy, whereas the organised, high-information state is associated with low entropy.*

To organise a system, to drive it away from equilibrium into a less disorderly state, requires work. The information content of

---

* This *inverse* relationship between information and entropy is in contrast to that initially proposed by Claude Shannon. The matter will be considered in detail in chapter 5.

a system may therefore be related to the amount of work required to create it. "Useful" work is defined here as the work which *decreases* the entropy of the universe in contrast to merely heating a gas, for example. Useful work performed upon a system, generally increases its thermodynamic improbability and increases its organisation. The application of useful work represents one way to increase the information content of a system. All systems worked upon, experience a change in entropy and in organisation. Hence work causes changes in the information content of a system – a relationship to be examined in detail in chapter 7. The present chapter will focus on the precise relationship between changes in entropy and changes in information.

The Second Law of Thermodynamics

The second law of thermodynamics considers that for any system, there exists a state of equilibrium towards which the system may change spontaneously; conversely, if there is a change in the system *away* from equilibrium, such a change can occur only at the expense of the displacement of another system towards equilibrium. If such a system proceeds in a given direction while opposed continuously by a force tending to reverse it, the system may be made to do useful work. It is possible to ascertain the maximum useful work obtainable from such a system: this quantity is termed the *change in free energy*, denoted by the symbols ΔF or ΔG. The magnitude of ΔG gives the maximum amount of work which may be obtained from the system under any given set of conditions.

The second law of thermodynamics is frequently expressed in the form of the equation:

$$\Delta G = \Delta H - T\Delta S \tag{3.1}$$

Where ΔH is the "enthalpy", the change in heat content at constant pressure, T is the absolute temperature, and S is the "entropy".

Entropy is one of the most misconstrued concepts encountered in the physical and engineering sciences. For a student entering the fields of science or engineering, there is not much difficulty in understanding the concepts associated with ΔG, ΔH, or T: *The free energy change* is representative of the maximum useful work obtainable, *the change in heat content* of the system is the result of the energy absorbed (or subtracted), and the absolute temperature appears to be a measure of the heat content of the system.*

With the possible exception of the relation between heat and temperature, which is frequently glossed over, all make sense. Not so for entropy. Entropy appears as an abstract mathematical quantity whose physical reality becomes impossible to visualise. The fact that changes in entropy may be measured precisely does not remove the shroud of mystery. Unlike heat, which may also be measured precisely, entropy is not perceivable to our physical senses. Entropy is so outside the range of common experience as to dumbfound all those who are unable or unwilling to believe in the reality of mathematical abstractions.

Entropy, in fact, is a mathematical expression describing disorder. It is not an expression of heat content, or its measure – temperature – although it is related to both.

That entropy is a function of the organisation of a system, rather than merely a function of its heat content (temperature), is illustrated in fig. 3.1 which plots the relationship between entropy and temperature in water.* Whereas much of the curve demonstrates a general correlation between temperature and entropy – ie, as temperature increases, entropy increases – there are two major discontinuities: one at around 273 K, the other at 373 K. These are of course the temperatures at which ice melts, and water turns to steam.

It is not mere coincidence that these dramatic rises in entropy, these obvious discontinuities, occur at exactly those temperatures where we can see before our very eyes such a profound change in the structure of matter (in this case water).

A further perusal of the fig. 3.1 confirms that entropy must be a function of disorganisation, or disorder, for it correlates with

---

* Actually, temperature measures the heat content per unit of mass. If the fundamental concepts of information physics prove to be correct, temperature is a direct measure of the heat content of the system. "Latent heat" or "heat of crystallisation" represent quantities related not to energy but to information. Latent heat is the energy needed to be supplied (or given up) in order to change matter from one organisational state to another. The question is discussed further in the next chapter.

---

* The author is indebted to D. Kaoukis for providing the computer plot used in this graph.

the increasingly random motion of the water molecules. It is this increasing randomness of motion which has, at times, led to the specious perception that entropy is a direct function of heat content. The application of heat to a body of matter causes the particles comprising the system to vibrate and to move at random with increasing velocity. However, such a process results in not one, but in two phenomena: an increase in the energy content of the system – measurable as an increase in temperature – and a decrease in the organisation of the system – measurable as an increase in entropy. Although the two, temperature and entropy, frequently go hand in hand, they represent quite different processes. This shows up clearly whenever one compares the changes in entropy with the changes in temperature in those regions where there occurs a major change in the structure of matter: A large change in entropy may be accompanied by a zero change in temperature.

Thus a change in entropy may be brought about not only by changing the heat content of the system, but also by changing its organisation: We may disorganise a system by applying heat, as

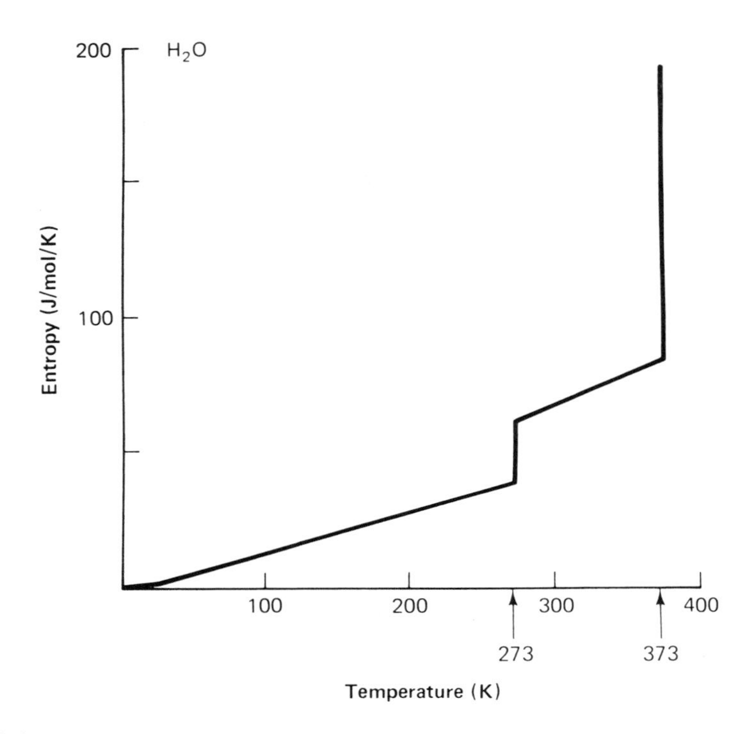

Fig. 3.1

when an ice cube melts by *withdrawing heat* from its surroundings. Alternatively, we may disorganise a system by altering its structure, as when a sugar cube is dissolved in water. Note that in this second case, the dissolving sugar cube is actually *releasing heat* to its surrounding.

In line with the basic postulate that organisation is a reflection of the information content of a system, we can state the following theorem:

The entropy of a system may be altered by altering either the heat content, or the organisation of the system. Either results in a change in the information content of that system.

The Boltzmann/Schrödinger Equation

If an increase in entropy represents a loss of organisation, ie, a loss of structural information, what then, is the precise relation between entropy and information? To explore this concept further let us begin with some interesting ideas suggested over 40 years ago by Erwin Schrödinger (1944) in his book *What is Life?*

Beginning with Boltzmann's investigations, Schrödinger considered (pp. 76–79) the statistical meaning of entropy. Boltzmann's equation, as stated by Schrödinger is:

$$\text{entropy} = k \log D \tag{3.2}$$

Where k is Boltzmann's constant, 3.2983×10^{-24} cal/deg, and D is a "quantitative measure of the atomistic disorder of the body in question".

Schrödinger goes on to state that the disorder D reflects: "partly that of heat motion, partly that which consists in different kinds of atoms or molecules being mixed at random, instead of being neatly separated, eg, ... sugar and water molecules". That is, the gradual diffusion of sugar throughout a body of liquid (as in a tea cup) represents an increase in the disorder D. Likewise, the addition of heat "increases the turmoil of heat motion", therefore increases the disorder D. Schrödinger stresses in particular that when you melt a crystal you "destroy the neat and permanent arrangement of the atoms and molecules and turn the crystal lattice into a continually changing random distribution".

The subtitle of Schrödinger's book is "The Physical Aspects of the Living Cell". Among other questions, he wonders how to express in statistical terms the tendency of living systems to maintain such low levels of entropy. He suggests that a living organism: "feeds upon negative entropy". He argues that if D is a measure of disorder, its reciprocal $1/D$ can be considered to be a direct measure of order. He therefore reformulates Boltzmann's equation as follows:

$$-(\text{entropy}) = k \log (1/D) \tag{3.3}$$

In other words: "entropy, taken with a negative sign, is itself a measure of order". In this manner does Schrödinger explain why an organism maintains its low levels of entropy. It does so by "sucking orderliness from its environment".

Information as an Inverse Exponential Function of Entropy

Schrödinger's equation (3.3) is our point of departure. We begin with Schrödinger's two assumptions: First, that disorder D is equivalent to Boltzmann's thermodynamic probability function W as expressed in Boltzmann's original equation.

$$S = k \log W \tag{3.4}$$

and second, that order is the reciprocal of disorder, ie:

$$Or = 1/D \tag{3.5}$$

where Or is a measure of the order of a system.

We now introduce a third assumption:
information I is a function of order:

$$I = f(Or) \tag{3.6}$$

Let us refine this third assumption by defining information such that it and organisation are directly and linearly related. This assumption is both necessary and reasonable: It is necessary because other assumptions lead to conceptual difficulties when assessing the changes in information content associated with changes in entropy. It is reasonable because just as the more matter a system contains, the greater its mass, so the more information a system contains, the greater its state of organisation. As we shall discuss in a later chapter, the quantity of information contained by a system is, at least in part, a function of the number of bonds linking the sub-units comprising the system into an organised whole (bonds which may be broken by heating the system or by dissolving it). However, at this point it suffices to make the assumption that information and organisation are directly and linearly related so that equation (3.6) may be stated as:

$$I = c(Or) \tag{3.7}$$

where c is a constant to be defined in the future.

Alternatively, we may consider order as a function of information, ie:

$$Or = I/c \tag{3.8}$$

which means:

$$D = 1/Or = c/I \tag{3.9}$$

By substituting in the original Boltzmann/Schrödinger equation (3.2) the term c/I we obtain:

$$S = k \log (c/I) \tag{3.10}$$

By solving for I, we obtain

$$I = ce^{-S/k} \tag{3.11}$$

Equations (3.10) and (3.11) define the fundamental relationship between information I and entropy S. A plot of this relationship is provided by fig. 3.2.

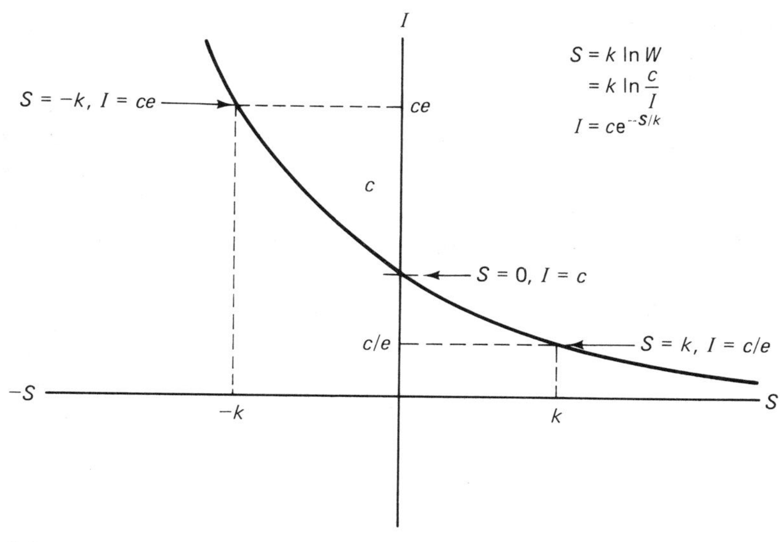

Fig. 3.2

The Constant c

Implicit in equation (3.1) and in fig. 3.2 is the fact that the constant c represents the information constant of the system at zero entropy.

For example, for a crystal of sodium chloride at 0 K,

$$c = I_o \tag{3.12}$$

where I_o is the information contained by the crystal at $S = 0$.

However, whereas c remains constant for all values of I and S within a system, it is not constant *across* systems.

This becomes intuitively apparent when one compares a single crystal such as that of sodium chloride, with a crystal of DNA. Surely at any comparable temperature below melting or dissociation, including at 0 K, the DNA will contain more information than the salt. Similarly, two gases – hydrogen (H_2) and oxygen (O_2) – will contain different amounts of information since the atoms comprising these two gases contain substantially different quantities of information : The hydrogen nucleus consists of a single proton while the oxygen nucleus consists of eight protons plus eight neutrons bound into a coherent unit. Therefore, at a ground stage of 0 K, the structural information contained by a perfect crystal of oxygen will be substantially more than the corresponding perfect crystal of hydrogen.

Equation (3.11) should therefore be expanded into a more generalised form, viz :

$$I = (I_o)\, e^{-S/k} \tag{3.13}$$

This difference in (I_o) would account for the fact that when two different gases are heated and allowed to expand, even under identical conditions of temperature and pressure, they still exhibit marked differences in entropy changes.

Returning to the Schrödinger/Boltzmann equation (3.2), ie, $S = k \log D$, in line with the above reasoning, the equation may be restated as

$$S = k \log [I_o/I] \tag{3.14}$$

which emphasises that the quantitative expression of disorder is the ratio between the information content of the system when its entropy is zero, and the actual information content of the system at any given entropic value S.

Such a ratio may be restated as a probability function, at which point its values correspond to Boltzmann's original W. It is important to realise that Boltzmann's equations were derived from a study of gases (Boltzmann 1896, 1898) in which I would never exceed I_o. Therefore S would never become negative. Furthermore, if one limits the analysis to order/disorder, one would also never observe S to acquire a negative value because once a system was "perfectly ordered" one could not add more order. Nothing could be more ordered than something which is already perfectly ordered. On the other hand, it would be quite possible to add more information to a system which is already perfectly ordered by making it more complex. To take a biological analogy, one could take a strand of perfectly ordered DNA and envelop it with a protein coat to produce a mature virus.

Literature Cited

L Boltzmann (1896, 1898) *Lectures on Gas Theory* Part I and Part II, translated by SG Brush, University of California Press, Berkeley, California, 1976.
E Schrödinger (1944) *What is Life?* Cambridge University Press.

· 4 ·

Measuring the Information Changes of Altered Physical States

Measuring the Information Content of a Crystal

The information content of a crystal may be analysed in terms of at least three components:

1. The information content of the individual sub-units – atoms or molecules – comprising the crystal.
2. The information content of the bonds which bind the sub-units into a "fixed" structure.
3. The resonances which a crystal exhibits and which contribute to its further organisation.

In addition there may be other information components such as nodes, antinodes and internodes. We will ignore these last for the moment on the assumption that either their information content is included in the first three components (particularly the resonances), or they are of second-order magnitude.

1. The information content of the sub-units may, in principle, be ascertained in the same way as the analysis applied to an entire crystal. Like a crystal, one may envisage an atom to be a complex structure consisting of nucleons and electrons organised into a coherent unit – while the nucleons, in turn, are comprised of sub-units (quarks) organised into coherent units.

Another approach would be to arbitrarily assign a value of unity to the hydrogen atom and expect the information content of other atoms to be a complex function of atomic mass.

However, as we shall see, this would lead to problems with the analysis of the information content of crystals, even though atomic mass must correlate positively, if not linearly, with information content.

2. The information content of the bonds which hold the sub-units in place may be calculated on the basis of entropy changes associated with a change in the physical state of the matter comprising the crystal. To be precise, the change in entropy between a perfect crystal at 0 K and its vapour state at the boiling point when all bonds have been broken and the atoms/molecules are acting as independent agents in a gas – will reflect the change in information content.

The change in entropy between a homogeneous material organised into a perfect crystal at 0 K, and its vapour phase at the boiling point may be stated as:

$$\Delta S = S_v - S_0 \tag{4.1}$$

Since the entropy at 0 K is 0, $S_0 = 0$,

$$\Delta S = S_v \tag{4.2}$$

If we make such a calculation for water, then at 373 K:

$$S_v = 200 \text{ J/K/mole (approximately)} \tag{4.3}$$

Or, per mole of water:

$$S_v = 200 \text{ J/K} \tag{4.4}$$

The formula derived earlier (chapter 3) from Schrödinger and Boltzmann on the relationship between information I and entropy S is:

$$I = (I_0)e^{-S/k} \tag{4.5}$$

where k is Boltzmann's constant, 1.38 × 10-23 J/K, and (I_0) is the information contained by the system at 0 K.

Per mole of water:

$$\begin{aligned} S/k &= (200 \text{ J/K}) \,/\, (1.38 \times 10^{-23} \text{ J/K}) \\ &= 1.45 \times 10^{25} \end{aligned} \tag{4.6}$$

Substituting (4.6) in (4.5)

$$I = (I_0)e^{-(1.45 \times 10)^{25}} \tag{4.7}$$

$$I = (I_0)\, 2^{-(2.1 \times 10)^{25}} \tag{4.8}$$

The increase in entropy associated with the increase in temperature shows up as a *negative sign* in the exponent of equation (4.8), indicating a *loss* of information.

Assuming that the exponent in equation (4.8) represents the changes in information as expressed by the changes in entropy, and because the exponent is to the base 2, assume that this exponent may be stated as bits, then the loss of information by boiling a perfect ice crystal may be stated as:

$$\log_2 I = \log_2 (I_0) - 2.1 \times 10^{25} \text{ bits/mole} \quad (4.9)$$

The converse statement of the above would be that in order to organise a mole of steam (at 373 K) into a perfect crystal of ice (at 0 K) would require an input of 2.1×10^{25} bits of information, or on average, of about 35 bits per molecule. The total information change, however, would involve the mathematical product of the change of information state as measured by changes in entropy, multiplied by I_0, the information contained by the individual water molecules. That is, even though the crystal has been destroyed, the individual water molecules still possess information.

3. In addition to the direct bonds which hold the sub-units together, eg, the electrostatic attraction between ions of opposite charge, a perfect crystal represents a resonating system which may involve standing waves, and one or more force fields which, although generated by the crystal itself, act on the sub-units as an externally imposed force. Such standing waves or fields will have nodes, antinodes and internodes which "force" the individual sub-units into organised geometric patterns.

The model for the above is the trapping of gaseous ions existing in a cloud-like state by means of a complex arrangement of electric and magnetic fields. The randomly moving ions become fixed by the externally imposed electromagnetic fields into a regular array, characteristic of the crystalline state (see for example, Wineland et al. 1987).

The extent of resonance which a crystal exhibits reflects, in part, how perfect it is. There is a range of crystalline states ranging from a powder at one extreme to a perfect crystal at absolute zero temperature. A measurement of this range is the sharpness of the peaks of X-ray diffraction patterns. That is, the greater the angle of the spread, the less perfect the crystal. Hence the less organised and the lower is its information content.

Another measure could be based on the extent to which superconductivity may be observed. Both resonance conductivity and superconductivity might constitute a measure of the extent of organisation (hence information content) of a crystal. This would be particularly relevant for crystals made up of heterogeneous sub-units such as perovskites whose electric properties have recently made them a focus of great interest because of high-temperature superconductivity (see review by Hazen 1988).

Measuring resonance may prove to be even more important when analysing crystals of organic molecules, particularly those which have evolved to function as electron transport molecules (eg, certain carotenoid and phenolic compounds). Inasmuch as boiling a perfect crystal also destroys the resonances and associated phenomena, the entropy change (ΔS) occurring between 0 and 373 K (for water), reflects not only the destruction of the bonds, as analysed in (2) above, but also the resonances. However, the considerations in this section (3) may allow one to measure the resonance and associated organisational features of a crystal (or polymer), such as nodes, etc, as distinct from the primary information content consisting of the bonds which fix the sub-units into an ordered matrix. Such measurements may also prove particularly fruitful when trying to ascertain the information content of sub-molecular and sub-atomic structures.

Proteins as Information Systems

Another system in which an expanding body of knowledge allows us to analyse the relationship between organisation and entropy is that of protein chemistry. The alphabet of proteins consists of amino acids. Just as the written English language consists of the 26 letters of the alphabet, plus some other notations (including the blank space between words), so in the case of human proteins, the language is based on approximately 20 amino acids, plus other bits and pieces.

All amino acids have one feature in common. They have a carbon atom which on one side is linked to an amino group (-NH2) and on the other side to an acid – a carboxyl group (-COOH). The other two bonds of this central carbon atom are taken up by a hydrogen atom H, and secondly, what is frequently referred to as an R group.

$$\begin{array}{c} \mathrm{R} \\ | \\ \mathrm{NH_2{-}CH{-}COOH} \end{array}$$

The R group determines the individual properties of each of the amino acids and may range from a second single hydrogen atom, to fairly exotic side chains containing benzene rings, sulphur atoms, and even more complex and varied structures. The R groups possess properties of great significance which will be considered shortly. First let us focus on the central carbon atom flanked by an amino group on one side, and a carboxyl group on the other. These two groups may be made to link up by a peptide bond (-CO-NH-). This type of linkage allows the carboxyl group of amino acid A to be linked to the amino group of amino acid B. The carboxyl group of amino acid B may now be linked to the amino group of amino acid C, and its carboxyl to D, etc. By this process polypeptides may be formed which are simply a string of amino acids.

$$\begin{array}{c} \quad R_1 \qquad\qquad R_2 \qquad\qquad R_3 \qquad\qquad\qquad R_n \\ NH_2\text{-}CH\text{-}CO\text{-}NH\text{-}CH\text{-}CO\text{-}NH\text{-}CH\text{-}CO\text{-} \ldots \text{-}NH\text{-}CH\text{-}COOH \end{array}$$

Some proteins are merely very large polypeptides involving chains made up of hundreds of amino acids. The specific sequence of amino acids determines the primary structure of a protein. That is, the primary structure of a protein depends on which amino acid follows which in the polypeptide chain.

The bonding angles of carbon and nitrogen preclude having the amino acids line up neatly in a flat plane. The chain of amino acids twists and the various side chains (the R groups) stick out in various directions. This is the basis for the secondary structure of a protein.

Chains of amino acids may curl back upon themselves. At this point some of the R groups sticking out on one side will link up with some of the other R groups on the main chain. This may put a permanent crimp in the main chain. A protein molecule may contain several such loops and folds. At this point, a protein, instead of being a simple linear chain, will have a decided three-dimensional structure. It is this folding of a twisted polypeptide chain into a complex three-dimensional molecule which represents the *tertiary* structure of the molecule.

Finally, two or more such tertiary chains of polypeptides may act as sub-units to combine into larger units. This, then, constitutes the *quarternary* structure of a large protein.

It must become apparent from the above description that just as the 26 letters of the English alphabet can give rise to an entire language of well over a hundred thousand words, so can twenty amino acids link up to combine into a hundred thousand different kinds of proteins. Actually, the number of proteins possible is very much larger because, whereas most words consist of less than 10 letters, most proteins consist of chains of hundreds of amino acids.

Some of these proteins are structural, for example, collagen which is an important constituent of connective tissues; another is elastin in ligaments. Others are combined with special, non-protein components to carry out special functions, such as haemoglobin transporting oxygen through the bloodstream. The largest group known, however, are enzymes. Enzymes are organic catalysts which contain the information necessary for making chemical reactions happen with a very much higher thermodynamic probability than one would expect, given the temperatures (and other physical parameters) of the cell system. Enzymes can take large molecules apart, and in the process extract useful energy. Alternatively, they can create large molecules (including proteins) from smaller sub-units (eg, amino acids). They provide the information for building big molecules, or for chopping them up. Most important, they are crucial for the flows of energy through, and the work produced by, living systems.

The Denaturation of Trypsin

Trypsin is an enzyme secreted by the pancreas to aid in the digestion of proteins. Its ready availability from the guts of slaughtered animals has meant that it was among the earliest of enzymes to be studied extensively. Although the enzyme was originally discovered and studied in relation to human and animal digestive tracts, it also proved to play a significant role at cellular and sub-cellular levels. The enzyme possesses a molecular mass of about 24,000 daltons. It acts by hydrolysing a peptide bond at those points in the polypeptide chain which contain either of the amino acids, arginine or lysine.

As with most enzymes, trypsin exhibits a high specifity for the three-dimensional atomic and electronic structure of the polypeptide chain at the site of attack. Both the enzyme (trypsin), and the substrate (eg, a peptide bond involving the amino acid arginine), possess a spatial organisation which allows the one to "recognise" the other as a proper "fit" – analogous to a complex lock and key. Enzymes, therefore, represent a major information input into the system (membranes represent another). An enzyme should be considered as a piece of information machinery which provides the information environment which allows a reaction to proceed at a much lower temperature. The enzyme lowers the activation energy.

A measure of the information contained in the tertiary structure of an enzyme can be ascertained by measuring the changes in entropy upon inactivating the protein by heating. Heating causes the enzyme to lose its characteristic tertiary structure. Most chemical reactions, involving a reactant in solution, are accompanied by changes in entropy of less than 60 cal/deg/mole. In contrast, the denaturation of the trypsin as it changes from a highly organised, biologically active compound, to a less organised, inactive state involves 213 cal/deg/mole (Fruton and Simmonds 1958, using data from Anson and Mirsky 1934). In other words, the difference in information between a molecule which works (as an enzyme), and one which does not, even though it is made up of virtually the same atoms (!), in the case of trypsin involves a change in entropy such that:

$$\Delta S = 213 \text{ cal/deg/mole}$$

As with the crystal of water, the ability to measure a significant change in the organisation of the trypsin molecule as a precisely quantifiable change in its entropy, allows one to express such a change in terms of a quantifiable change in information:*

I	$S =$	$k \ln W$	(Boltzmann's equation)	(4.10)
	$S_n =$	$k \ln W_n$	(n = native protein)	(4.11)
	$S_d =$	$k \ln W_d$	(d = denaturated protein)	(4.12)
II	$\Delta S =$	$S_d - S_n$		(4.13)
	$=$	$k \ln W_d - k \ln W_n$		(4.14)
	$=$	$k [\ln W_d - \ln W_n]$		(4.15)
	$=$	$k \ln [W_d/W_n]$		(4.16)
	$\Delta S/k =$	$\ln [W_d/W_n]$		(4.17)
III	$\Delta S =$	213 cal/K/mole	(Fruton & Simmonds)	(4.18)
	$=$	891 J/K/mole	(1 J = 0.239 cal)	(4.19)
	1 mole $=$	6.03×10^{23} molecules	(Avogadro's constant)	(4.20)
	$\Delta S =$	147.8×10^{-23} J/K/molecule		(4.21)
	$k =$	1.38×10^{-23} J/K	(Boltzmann's constant)	(4.22)

* The author is indebted to Dr. N. McEwen for introducing him to these calculations.

$$\Delta S/k = 107.1/\text{molecule} \quad (4.23)$$
$$\text{IV} \quad \ln W_d/W_n = \Delta S/k \quad (\text{from } 4.17) \quad (4.24)$$
$$= 107.6/\text{molecule} \quad (\text{from } 4.23) \quad (4.25)$$
$$W_d/W_n = e^{107.6} \text{ per molecule} \quad (4.26)$$
$$= 5.4 \times 10^{46}/\text{molecule} \quad (4.27)$$
$$\doteqdot 2^{155}/\text{molecule} \quad (4.28)$$
$$\text{V} \quad W_d = c/I_d \quad (\text{by definition, see chapter 3}) \quad (4.29)$$
$$W_n = c/I_n \quad (4.30)$$
$$W_d/W_n = [c/I_d]/[c/I_n] \quad (4.31)$$
$$= I_n/I_d \quad (4.32)$$
$$\text{VI} \quad I_n/I_d \doteqdot 2^{155} \text{ per molecule} \quad (\text{from } 4.28) \quad (4.33)$$

Equations (4.26), (4.27), and (4.28) express the increase in thermodynamic probability associated with the denaturation of a molecule of enzyme. This change is represented as a ratio of the probability associated with each of the two states of protein organisation. Equation (4.33) does the same as equation (4.28) but in terms of the ratio of structural information changes.

The exponent of this ratio, $I_n{:}I_d = 2^{155}$/molecule, could be interpreted as representing an information change involving 155 bits per molecule. This value does not tell us the absolute value of the information contained by the two forms of protein. Nevertheless, it hints at the enormous magnitude of the information change as a native protein molecule loses its tertiary structure. The implication is that for a single molecule of denatured trypsin to regain its effective native state, it would need to traverse a binary decision tree about 155 nodes deep. With such a conceptualisation it becomes possible to restate equation (4.33) in terms of bits of information:

$$\log_2 I_d \doteqdot \log_2 I_n - 155 \text{ bits per molecule} \quad (4.34)$$

In other words, in order to organise a heteropolymer molecule consisting of a chain of amino acid into a functioning enzyme by folding the chain into its three-dimensional, tertiary structure, requires an addition of information equivalent to 155 bits.

Concluding Remarks

Highly organised aperiodic crystals such as proteins show large changes in organisation long before the sub-units are vapourised. Note that whereas it takes only 35 bits of information to condense water vapour into a perfect ice crystal, it takes 155 bits merely to fold the trypsin polypeptide chain (already possessing a primary and secondary polymer structure) into a functioning enzyme molecule.

Finally, if the assumptions made earlier prove to be correct, such that the bits per molecule lost when a perfect ice crystal is vaporised (35), or a trypsin molecule is denatured (155), then one may calculate that an entropy change of approximately 6 J/K/mole is required to bring about a loss, on average of one bit per *molecule*, or conversely:

One entropy unit equals approximately 10^{23} bits/mole.

If this is true, then per degree, one joule of energy is equivalent to approximately 10^{23} bits of information, ie,

$$1 \text{ J/K} = 10^{23} \text{ bits} \qquad (4.35)$$

Literature Cited

JS Fruton and S Simmonds (1958) *General Biochemistry*, John Wiley, New York.

RM Hazen (1988) Perovskites, *Sci. Am.* 258(6):52–61.

DJ Wineland, JC Bergquist, WM Itano, JJ Bollinger and CH Manney (1987) Atomic-ion coulomb clusters in an ion trap, *Phys. Rev. Lett.* 59(26):2935–2938.

· 5 ·

Information and Entropy: Further Implications

Introduction

The mathematical relationship between information and entropy described in the preceding chapters requires further paradigm shifts in at least four areas:

1. The relationship defined by equations (3.10) and (3.11) flies in the face of the relationship as traditionally defined by the communications engineers.
2. The equations imply that entropy may have a negative value, as indicated in fig. 3.2.
3. The exponential growth of the curve in the upper left quadrant of the graph (fig. 3.2) indicates that the values for information I grow extremely large for very small negative changes in entropy. Furthermore, there is no theoretical upper limit for information.
4. Although entropy may be increasing throughout the universe, so is information. The universe, rather than ending up as a uniform soup of particles with very low energies – the entropic death – may instead, end up in a state in which all matter and energy have been converted into pure information.

Let us examine these implications more closely.

Information and Entropy as Viewed by the Communications Engineers

The idea that information and entropy are somehow related has been around for some time. Leo Szilard in a paper in 1929 embarked on an exploration of Maxwell's demon which could sort out the "swifter molecules" from the slower ones in a chamber of gas. Szilard considered that the demon possessed information about the molecules of gas and was converting information into a form of negative entropy.*

It was the communications engineering field which first saw the utility of applying the idea of entropy to the transmission of information. Claude Shannon (1948), in his classic treatise "A mathematical theory of communication" related information to entropy. However, the concepts elucidated by Shannon and co-workers differ markedly from those discussed in the present exploration. Shannon never claimed to have developed a theory of information. As indicated in the title of his original work, he was interested in developing a mathematical theory of *communication*. However, Shannon did treat the "information" being communicated as an abstract, quantifiable entity. It is not unnatural therefore, that since the information being transmitted could be handled mathematically, the impression grew that Shannon had devised a theory of information. This was unfortunate.

Colin Cherry (1978, pp. 43–44) has reviewed the earlier (1928) work of R.V.L. Hartley, who defined information as the successive selection of signs or words from a given list. Hartley, concerned with the *transmission* of information, rejected all subjective factors such as meaning, since his interest lay in the transmission of signs or physical signals. As such, he could show that a message of N signs chosen from an alphabet of S signs,

---

* In the real world, biological systems utilising membranes are filled with such demons at work: For example, the green alga *Valonia* consists of a hollow sphere with liquid inside. This liquid is known to contain concentrations of potassium a thousand-fold greater than the surrounding sea water. Similarly the human kidney is continuously sorting out molecules from the blood, excreting the potentially harmful ones (including excess water). A kidney requires energy in order to perform its work. As such, it is one of many examples of biological machines which convert energy into information. That is, biological demons perform the work of Maxwell's demons – sorting molecules and decreasing entropy – but do so only as a result of an input of energy.

has S^N possibilities. Furthermore, the "quantity of information" could, most reasonably, be defined as the logarithm:

$$H = N \log S \quad (5.1)$$

It was on this, and related ideas, that Shannon formulated his concepts. As Colin Cherry has commented [p. 51]: "it is a pity that the mathematical concepts stemming from Hartley have been called 'information' at all". The formula derived by Shannon for the average information in a long sequence of n symbols, is:

$$H_n = - p_i \log p_i \quad (5.2)$$

As Cherry points out: "H_n is really a measure of one facet only of the concept of information; it is the statistical rarity or 'surprise value' of a course of message signs."

To confuse matters further, in his analysis of the statistical behaviour of symbols in a message, Shannon used the concept of entropy as a metaphor. For example, Shannon and Weaver (1964, p. 12) state that "The quantity which uniquely meets the natural requirements that one sets up for 'information' turns out to be exactly that which is known in thermodynamics as *entropy*" [italic in original text]. They point out [p. 13] "That information be measured by entropy is, after all, natural when we remember that information, in communication theory, is associated with the amount of freedom of choice we have in constructing messages." Shannon and Weaver therefore consider that a situation which is highly organised "is not characterised by a large degree of randomness or of choice, that is to say, the information (or the entropy) is low".

In a thoughtful discussion of the relationship between entropy and information, Jeffrey Wicken (1987) points out [p. 179]: "While the Shannon equation is symbolically isomorphic with the Boltzmann equation, the meanings of the respective equations bear little in common." In thermodynamics, the macrostate is what is empirically measurable; the microstate is a theoretical construct. The microstate may possess physical reality but individual microstates cannot be measured. It is in this sense that a microstate is different from a message. A message is concrete and definable; in contrast, the set of all possible messages which might have been sent, sensible and nonsensical – that is the theoretical construct [p. 180]. Shannon should have confined the term "entropy" to a property of the ensemble rather than extending it to the message itself. The

Shannon formula measures the complexity of structural relationships. However, the formula required to specify a structure does quantify the information *content*. Nonsense sequences or structures require as much information for a quantitative definition as do those which carry functional meaning [pp. 184–185].

The idea that information and entropy are the same, was subsequently replaced with the idea that information was equivalent to negentropy. Leon Brillouin, in his book *Science Information Theory*, defines negentropy simply as the negative of entropy and states that [p. 154] "information can be changed into negentropy, and that information ... can be obtained only at the expense of the negentropy of some physical system". This version of the Shannon/Weaver approach has tended to permeate other areas of information theory. Stafford Beer (1972), well known for his cybernetics of organisation, has defined negentropy as [p. 306] "equalling the active information content of a system".

Brillouin's concept was designed to help overcome an anomaly in Shannon's theory: The more random is the arrangement of symbols – ie, the higher the entropy – the greater the information content. Taken to its logical extreme this would mean that pure noise, which contains the greatest amount of entropy, would contain the greatest amount of information. Shannon and Weaver were aware of this problem [Weaver p. 27]: "The concept of information developed in this theory at first seems disappointing and bizarre – disappointing because it has nothing to do with meaning, and bizarre because ... the two words *information* and *uncertainty* find themselves to be partners." The justification for this, as stated by Shannon [p. 31], is that the "semantic aspects of communication are irrelevant to the engineering problem. The significant aspect is that the actual message is one *selected from a set* of possible messages. The system must be designed to operate for each possible selection, not just the one which will actually be chosen". Shannon, the telephone engineer, was interested in defining the problems associated with moving information down a communications channel, not with information as a property of the universe. This then, is the discrepancy between the "information theory" derived from Hartley, Shannon and Weaver, and the neo-Shannonites such as Brillouin, on the one hand, and the concepts developed in the present work, on the other.

It should be emphasised, that the mathematical treatment by Shannon of quantities of symbols, and how to add them up, is not at issue here. The mathematical treatment of the syntactical aspects of language is most useful. However, Shannon's use of entropy as a metaphor is unfortunate. A physical relationship between information and entropy actually does exist. However, it is neither the direct relationship envisaged by Shannon, nor its negative as envisaged by Brillouin. For reasons discussed in the preceding chapters, physical information relates to order, and as Schrödinger has shown, order varies *inversely* with Boltzmann's thermodynamic probability function. Changes in the entropy of a physical system, therefore, do reflect changes in the information content of that system. However, the relationship involves an *inverse exponent*.

Furthermore, useful as Shannon's mathematics may be for assessing syntactical aspects of language, they are useless for analysing semantic aspects. The "meaning" of words is a function of "context". This involves analysing the "information environment" of a particular word or other semantic unit. An entirely different sort of mathematical treatment is required to achieve this – a matter to be examined in a subsequent work (*Beyond Chaos: Towards a General Theory of Information*).

Positive Entropy

Figure 3.2 shows that as entropy S increases, information I decreases. As entropy approaches infinity, information approaches zero.

It may be difficult to envisage how a gas consisting of molecules moving at random could possess any information whatsoever. The curve relating information to entropy should rapidly drop to zero I as one moves to the right along the S-axis, rather than being asymptotic with it.

However, a gas consists of molecules, and molecules contain information. The organisation intrinsic to molecules affects their behaviour as a gas. This is why two different gases heated equally under standard conditions will, nevertheless, exhibit different increments of entropy changes. Heating a gas may increase the speed at which the molecules move, but such an increase causes only a marginal increase in the randomisation (disorder). Hence a loss of organisation at the *inter*molecular level is minimal. At the *intra*molecular level, the internal structure of the molecules is not affected. Hence the total loss of information is slight.

On heating a gas further, however, there will occur discontinuities at which there may be observed large jumps in entropy associated with the destruction of organisation at more fundamental levels (see review by Greiner and Stocker 1985). The first of these involves the ionisation of gases as the intensity of molecular collision causes electrons to be knocked off and atoms to be dissociated. For example, steam, heated to 1,000 °C, becomes a plasma of ions and electrons. At higher energy levels, the integrity of the atoms themselves becomes compromised: In the normal ground state of matter the atomic nucleus is like a liquid droplet with the nucleons moving about freely within it but seldom straying beyond its surface. With sufficiently high energy applications, nuclear matter is observed to "boil". At higher temperatures still, the nucleons themselves become disorganised to yield a plasma of quarks and gluons (a quagma).

Of particular interest is the relation of entropy to these transformations. The effect of entropy on the mass spectrum has been used by a team at Michigan State University to measure the entropy produced in collisions. The team found a considerably higher increase in the entropy produced in particle collisions at intermediate energies than would be expected from calculations based on the properties of normal nuclear matter. Lazlo P. Csernai of the University of Minesota has suggested that the extra entropy may reflect the transition from a liquid to a vapour, and has described the sequence of events which could lead to such an observation.

The hydrodynamic model of heavy-ion collisions relies on thermodynamic concepts. These assume that particles in motion move randomly. It is by no means certain that this condition is satisfied inside nuclear matter. That is, the particles may well interact with each other. However, gas molecules in traditional thermodynamic systems are assumed to be ideal, ie, they do not interact with each other. This is obviously not the case in the real world. Therefore, even if nuclear particles do interact, that need not negate a thermodynamic analysis. The unexplained increase in entropy of nuclear reactions are most probably associated with the break-up of organised bodies.

The latent heat absorbed when ice melts, reflects the extra heat required to convert a crystalline structure to a liquid. The same is true when liquid water evaporates. Such points along the heat/temperature curve in which one observes a discontinuity in the relationship between the application of heat, the rise in temperature (or lack of it), and the increase in entropy, are always associated with basic changes in the organisation of matter. This principle applies not only to changes in intermolecular organisation, but also to sub-molecular, sub-atomic, and sub-nuclear organisation.

In the light of the above, one would expect the "zero information/infinite entropy" state to be approached when the system consists of a plasma of pure fundamental particles containing no organisation whatsoever (at neither the inter- nor at the intra-particle level). The "zero information/infinite entropy" state would be *achieved* when even the fundamental particles are transformed (evaporated?) into pure energy. At this point the addition of further energy would have no further impact on the organisation of matter, since matter would no longer exist. In other words, the "infinite entropy" state not only would comprise a zero information state, but also a zero matter state. In addition, the infinite entropy state would allow no organisation to be exhibited by energy, therefore the fundamental forces of nature would also disappear. Current cosmological theories consider such a condition to have existed inside the big bang at time zero. The implications for cosmology will be considered later.

Negative Entropy

The laws of thermodynamics are as applicable to chemical and biological systems as they are to physical systems. However, biological systems are profoundly different from physical systems. Given that there is a constant input of energy into biological systems from a distant source (the sun), it is not unnatural that the biological scientist frequently encounters reactions in the system under study in which the entropy continually decreases. The biologist is not concerned about the fact that such a process can occur only at the expense of the sun running down (thereby increasing the total entropy of the universe). The biologist's daily dose of experiencing the accumulation of negative entropy in the system under study, obviously leads to a different outlook on the matter from the physicist/engineer who almost never observes it. Therefore it comes as no surprise to a biological scientist that the curve plotting the relationship between information and entropy indicates that whereas information always remains positive, entropy may become negative. This raises the question: Is it possible for entropy to exist in a negative state, and if so, what is negative entropy?

Entropy measures the randomisation or disorganisation of matter. The entropy contained in matter may be reduced in one of two ways: (1) By withdrawing heat, or (2) by adding information. If all possible heat were to be withdrawn from a system, its temperature would be 0 K, and according to Nernst, its entropy would also be zero. This has been designated as the Third Law of Thermodynamics.

Information physics would modify this law: If one accepts that entropy is a measure of organisation, being inversely related, then at 0 K, there is nothing to keep the system from becoming even more organised by adding more information. That is, whereas it becomes impossible to withdraw more heat from a system which is at 0 K, making it impossible to further reduce entropy (to a negative value) by the further *withdrawal of heat*, there is no theoretical reason why one may not further decrease entropy by the *addition of information*. Just as in the case of Fahrenheit, temperature may go below 0°F – Fahrenheit having picked that point as the coldest achievable in his day – so may entropy go below the zero point Nernst picked on the basis of his investigations.

To the crystallographer, the physical scientist, and the engineer, the idea of adding information to a perfect crystal at 0 K in order to achieve negative entropy may seem fanciful – firstly, since it appears to violate the traditional concepts of entropy – it appears intuitively false; and secondly, there seems to be no way of achieving this feat anyhow, therefore it would have no obvious application or predictive value. However, suppose one could invent a force field which would "freeze" the atoms and their constituents – electrons and nucleons – into total immobility, even at room temperature. There is no theoretical reason why such a system might not, some day, be invented.

In fact, we can identify two known phenomena which approximate such force fields able to hold atoms (though not electrons) in a relatively immobile state at elevated temperatures. The first is exemplified by the work of Wineland et al. (1987), in which vaporised ions of mercury, although in a gaseous state, are made to conform to a crystalline state by confining the ions in a Paul radio-frequency trap. The second phenomenon involves organic molecules in which the resonating pi cloud of electrons acts as an interatomic force stabilising the positions of the atoms. We will return to the phenomenon of organic molecules, shortly.

If, to the physical scientist or engineer, negative entropy seems implausible, to the knowledge engineer trying to develop a general theory of information, the situation looks both plausible and interesting: Instead of contemplating an array of physical particles organised into a crystal, let us consider an array of human symbols organised into a definite symbolic structure – letters of the Latin alphabet (plus relevant punctuation symbols) organised into a sentence. In such a case, it becomes easy to see how, starting with a zero entropy state, one can add information and reduce entropy further to an absolute negative value.

To do so, we need to return to Shannon's information theory and have another look at the isomorphism between his equation and the entropy equation. Wicken (1987), referring to the work of Brush (1983) points out that Boltzmann and Shannon were independently using equations which had already been applied to games of chance a century earlier by the French mathematician DeMoivre. As Wicken points out [p. 179], each equation deals with *uncertainties*; or as Colin Cherry [p. 51] has pointed out in Shannon's case, H_n represents the statistical rarity, or "surprise value" of a string of message signs.

In Boltzmann's case

$$S = k \log W \tag{5.3}$$

W represents the total number of microstates possible in a given physical system, where each microstate defines the energy state of a given particle . Atoms moving around in a gas possess a larger number of possible microstates than atoms tied into a crystalline structure. At 0 K, all microstates become identical since all possess zero energy – there can exist only a single microstate, ie, $W = 1$. Therefore $S = 0$.

Boltzmann's W, therefore, is a measure of the disorder created by heat. Insofar as Boltzmann's equation deals with the *energy* content of microstates, the equation cannot be used to examine possible entropy states less than zero: One cannot have less energy than the zero energy state at 0 K. In contrast, Schrödinger's modification of Boltzmann's equation, which emphasises not only disorder, but also order, places no such limitations on entropy. If a way could be found to further organise the system ... then the entropy could be reduced further.

The reduction, below zero entropy in a linguistic situation becomes comprehensible if we look at the possible strings of letters comprising a sentence. Shannon's equation allows one to calculate the number of strings of letters possible, given a fixed number of letters to choose from. (Note, to simplify the argument, the term "letter" in the present discussion denotes all message signs of the written English language including punctuation marks and spaces between words.)

$$H_n = -\sum_i P_i \log P_i \qquad (5.4)$$

Shannon's average information content H_n shrinks to zero if the number of possible letter combinations P_i is restricted to a single combination.

It is true, as emphasised earlier, that Shannon's number of possible states achieved by stringing together a variety of letters, is not the same as Boltzmann's number of possible microstates achieved by imbueing particles with varying quantities of energy. Nevertheless, both deal with *the mathematics of uncertainty*. Both equate an increase in entropy with an increase in uncertainty. Boltzmann ties the increase in entropy of a physical system to an increase in its thermodynamic probability. Shannon (with Weaver) ties the increase in the entropy of a message to greater degrees of freedom and hence to a greater "information" content. For both, the base line of zero is achieved when the number of states is reduced to a single (fixed) state. In Shannon's case, any given string of letters, once on paper, or spoken into a telephone, eliminates all other possibilities. At that point in space and time, P_i is reduced to 1. Once a sequence of letters has been specified, we are no longer dealing with uncertainty. For Boltzmann, the same may be said for a perfect crystal at 0 K.

Thus in both instances, thermodynamic and linguistic, *the elimination of uncertainty provides us with a base line of zero entropy*.

Let us now examine two strings of letters. Both would be specified, and both would lack uncertainty; therefore neither would contain any entropy, ie, $S = 0$. However, the first string is gibberish in the English language, being the result of randomly choosing a string of, let us say, 27 letters plus 4 spaces (followed by a period). The second string, utilising the same 27 letters, is a sentence with meaning to the average reader able to read English.

(S1) Evaaye dter pfa celbu sleheoarl.
(S2) Please read the above carefully.

Why does the second contain more information than the first? The answer is simply this: More work has gone into S2 than S1. Using the same raw materials – the twenty-six letters of the English alphabet (upper and lower case) the space between letters, and the punctuation marks – S2 has undergone substantially more *information processing* than S1 because S2 involved ordering the letters in relation to a meaningful context!

In contrast, contemporary "information theory" derived from Shannon would consider S2 to contain *less* information than S1, it would consider S2 to have less "entropy" than S1. The neo-Shannonite argument would be "proved" by showing a person the first letter of the sentence, then asking them to guess the second. After establishing the second letter, asking them to guess the third, and so on until all 27 letters and 4 spaces had been correctly entered. An English-speaking reader would quickly pick up a pattern in the sequence of letters and spaces in S2 because of its semantic content – it would make sense to the reader. S1, on the other hand, would make no sense and would require many guesses for each of the blank spaces. For the neo-Shannonites this would mean that S1 had a much greater "surprise value", therefore would contain both more "entropy" and more "information".

As discussed earlier, the theory of information expounded in the present work, would agree that the entropy in S1 is greater than that of S2: However, it rejects the idea that S1 has *more* information because it contains greater uncertainty. On the contrary, S1 has less information because it lacks the obvious patterns of linguistic organisation which characterise S2. Only if it could be proved that S1 contains a code and that it involved greater information processing to achieve, could one consider S1 to contain more information.

As a counter to the neo-Shannonite "proof", one could ask someone not familiar with an Indo-European language, but familiar with the Latin alphabet – for example a Finn – to play the same game. To the Finn, the "surprise value" encountered in S2 will be at least as great as in S1. Thus by neo-Shannonite argument, the information content of S2 has increased. It would now equal, perhaps even surpass that of S1 (S1 looks more Finnish than English). Yet it is the same sentence! No coherent theory of information can be constructed on such shifting grounds.

Both S1 and S2 involved a significant amount of information processing. S1 required a system (human or machine) whose memory included a data base of the Latin alphabet and associated message symbols as described above. It then had to pick a certain number of them. The instruction could have been: Obtain 27 letters, print them out at random in a series of six–four–three–five–nine letter words and place a period at the end. In fact, even these instructions, leading to a 27-letter gibberish sentence, would have led to any number of such sentences, but not S1. The instructions would have to be much more precise, and very lengthy. A lot of information would have to be expended to duplicate the exact sequence of letters in S1. However, S1 is merely the product of the author's whim. A gibberish sentence such as S1 could be produced by any non-English speaking person who had been presented with a Latin alphabet; or S1 could be produced by a computer instructed to do so.

How very different is the story with S2: Its author would have learned the English language, understood the meanings of words, chosen the words from the many tens of thousands available in the author's head, chosen the letters to create the words, decided on the appropriateness of the sequence of words to the context of the present discussion, and conducted the many forms of information processing of which the human brain is capable.

The brain, in order to think, expends substantial amounts of energy. It is said that a student in deep concentration while taking an examination expends as much energy as a student jogging along at a fairly good speed. Furthermore, consider the enormous amount of work expended during the lifetime of the author, organising information to create a mental model of the world, as well as developing the tools of reading and writing. It is not only the information processing of the moment which characterises the degree of organisation of S2 – it is the entire history of the author and the author's culture which contributed to S2. Such an information history (data base?) is not required to create a gibberish sentence such as S1.

To return to our consideration of negative entropy. S1 contains certainty; its entropy is zero. S2 not only contains certainty, but has had added to it a great deal more work in the form of refined information processing. Keeping in mind the inverse relationship between information and entropy, the added information content of S2 means that it must contain *less* entropy than S1. Since S1 contained zero entropy, S2 must contain *negative* entropy.

Molecules such as DNA and proteins, consist of strings of simpler molecules (nucleotides, amino acids). Such sequences represent a series of messages. If such substances are placed within the *context* of a cell, they may have "meaning" for that cell – for example, the cell may duplicate the message encoded in the DNA. Thus more information units are created and the entropy within the cell declines further.

Biological systems, therefore, are somewhere between inorganic crystals at 0 K, and human symbolic systems. The evolution of all living systems involves a continuous increase in the information content of such systems. It is this phenomenon – the continuous decrease in the entropy of living systems, which caused Schrödinger to ponder. In a subsequent work (*Beyond Information*) the present author intends to examine the relationship between intelligence (all biological systems exhibit some measure of intelligence) and the negation of entropy.

To return to a physical system such as a crystal, there is another way in which to conceptualise the possibility that entropy may fall below zero: Envisage a structure thermodynamically more *improbable* than a perfect crystal at absolute zero. What might be more improbable than such a crystal? For one thing, a perfect crystal at room temperature. Although the matter has not been properly investigated, organic systems exhibit properties which would be associated with inorganic crystals near absolute zero. First, the covalent bonds and other linkages such as pi electrons stabilise interatomic linkages of highly organised and complex matter into tightly bound structures. That is, at temperatures well above 0 K, the restriction of the freedom of movement of atoms in an organic molecule is equal to that of an inorganic crystal at 0 K. This restriction of movement in an organised organic crystal such as a protein molecule accounts for the large changes in entropy upon its disorganisation.

The second phenomenon involves superconductivity. It has become apparent in recent decades that between 0 K and the melting point of certain substances, there may exist another thermodynamic state: that associated with superconductivity – a product of thermal and electromagnetic resonance phenomena. The destruction of superconductivity as a result of heating is as real a phase transition as that associated with melting ice, or vapourising water.

For most inorganic systems, superconductivity occurs at temperatures close to absolute zero. Again, the matter has not been properly investigated but A. Szent-Gyorgyi (1968 p. 23) has suggested that the function of a molecule such as carotene is to facilitate the movement of electrons with a minimum of energy loss.

Certainly, if one looks at the electronic resonance structures not only of the carotenoids, but also of phenolics, chlorophyll, haemoglobin, membranes, and other such systems, found in abundance in all cells, coupled to the insights biochemists have achieved in elucidating a myriad of metabolic electron transport systems, it would seem highly probable that many organic molecules and systems behave like superconducting systems at the usual (elevated) biological temperatures.

Present-day biological systems, with minor exceptions (eg, certain chemosynthetic bacteria), obtain their energy directly or indirectly from the sun. Light, as we shall discuss later, is a form of energy with a high information component. In general, biological systems eschew heat – either as an energy input, or as a product. When heat is generated, it is the by-product of metabolic reactions and usually reflects an inefficiency in the system. The one clear exception is the production of heat to maintain constant temperature in warm-blooded animals. This requirement for constant temperature undoubtedly reflects the increased efficiency of advanced metabolic systems operating in a highly organised environment. To maintain the very high levels of structural information in the system, the changes in entropy associated with changes in temperature must be kept to a minimum. The most advanced information processing system known is the mammalian brain. When the temperature rises only slightly above a critical threshold (as with a high fever), the system begins to fail as the individual hallucinates. A relatively slight drop in temperature, on the other hand, leads to narcosis. Thus even relatively minor (heat-induced) changes in entropy, change the delicate organisation of the system so as to interfere with effective information processing.

Therefore, in the one exception where biological systems do produce and utilise heat, the *function* of the added heat is not to provide energy, but to maintain a stable temperature so as to minimise externally induced entropy changes. In other words, heat is used to help stabilise organisation – it is one instance where the controlled application of heat constitutes an input of information.

Another, which involves an inorganic, physical system, the Bénard instability, will be discussed in chapter 6.

Physicists, in the past, have focussed on the running down of the universe – ultimately leading to "entropic death", a complete randomisation with no structure left. Biologists, on the other hand, have been observing the opposite – the evolution of increasingly complex systems. For biologists, virtually every system they study has increased in organisational complexity with evolution. Whether they look at DNA and related genetic systems, metabolic systems, cellular organisation, the organisation of organs such as the heart or the brain, the evolution of organisms, ecosystems, or the biosphere, the process is the same: Simple systems become more complex, more differentiated, more integrated, both within the system and with the environment outside the system – in short, biological systems evolve to become thermodynamically increasingly improbable.

The rest of the universe may be running down towards a state of maximum entropy, but (with the help of the sun) on this planet entropy is continually *decreasing*! This is true not only of biological systems, but it becomes even more apparent when one looks at cultural evolution, technological culture, and the evolution of human information systems. It is only in closed systems that entropy never decreases. In open systems, the entropy may not only decrease, it becomes much less than the zero point defined by Nernst.

Information Magnitudes

The fact that I as an exponential inverse function of S may involve ridiculous magnitudes should not deter us. The thermodynamic probability of highly organised structures with large amounts of negative entropy occurring spontaneously at temperatures well above 0 K must be infinitesimal. For example, the denaturation of trypsin discussed in the previous chapter could be interpreted to involve an increase in probability of the order of 155 bits per molecule, and that merely involves a change in the tertiary organisation of the protein, not its secondary or primary structures, which contain much more information still.

For example, consider the number of polypeptide chains possible in a modest-sized protein whose chain contains 200 amino acids: As discussed earlier, Hartley's formula states that a message of N signs chosen from an alphabet of S signs has S^N possibilities. Restricting our protein to being composed of the 21 essential amino acids only, we arrive at 21^{200} possible primary protein structures. In binary terms that would be equivalant to approximately 878 bits/molecule.

As a contrast, even if the English language consisted of only very long, ten-letter words, the total vocabulary possible would amount to 26^{10} (approximately one hundred million million possible words). Such a vocabulary would require only about 47 bits to describe any ten-letter word.

It is said that the longest word in the English dictionary is "antidisestablishmentarianism", consisting of 28 letters. Even if we made the ridiculous assumption that the entire English language consisted primarily of 30-letter words, it would still require less than 150 bits/word to describe them. In contrast, in the real world, there exist innumerable proteins much larger than ones containing a chain of 200 amino acids. For some, it would require *thousands* of bits to describe the primary structures of such molecules. Added to that are the secondary and tertiary structures. In addition, such polypeptide chains may aggregate to form the quaternary structures, and/or associate with other polymers to form glycoproteins, lipoproteins, or other complex crystals.

Obviously *proteins carry a vastly larger store of information than do human languages*. Proteins are only one of many information systems within living cells. Lipids, sugars, amino sugars, etc, to form membranes, starch, glycogen, cellulose, and many other polymers may be equally complex. DNA, the carrier of the genetic information, is, of course, more powerful still. A chain of 5,000 nucleotides represents $4^{5,000}$ possible combinations (the alphabet of DNA consists of four different nucleotides). It would require 10,000 bits/molecule to describe such chains.

Finally, the above represents only the raw material comprising living matter. The polymers discussed above, aggregate into complex, integrated macromolecular entities, which in turn, are somehow integrated into a functioning primitive (procaryotic) cell. That is, the discussion in the preceding paragraphs deals with information magnitudes at least two levels lower in complexity (and improbability) than that exhibited by the simplest of known cells – cells lacking nuclei and most organelles, and cells incapable of differentiating or organising into anything other than strings or clumps of such cells.

The orders of magnitude of improbability are huge. One may be able to put them into better perspective by making a calculation on the probability of finding the first living cell that appeared in this universe: Assume that a spherical part of the universe with a diameter of a billion light years originates the first living cell somewhere within it. The cell, 10 μm on edge, occupies a volume of $10^3\ \mu m^3$. Given a random sample of cubes of that dimension, what is the probability of finding that cell on the first shot?

$$\begin{aligned} r &= 0.5 \times 10^9 \text{ light year} \\ &= 0.5 \times 10^{22} \text{ kilometres} \\ &= 0.5 \times 10^{31} \text{ micrometres} \end{aligned}$$

$$V = \tfrac{4}{3} \pi r^3$$

$$V = 10^{93}\ \mu m^3 \text{ (approximately)}$$

This figure divided by $10^3\ \mu m^3$ gives us a probability of finding it on the first try of about one in 10^{90} tries.

The figure of about one in 10^{90} does not give a hint of the probability of the cell arising in the first place, merely the problem of finding it. When describing the information content of living systems, one will need to speak not of orders of magnitude, but of orders of decamagnitude, hectamagnitude, kilomagnitude, megamagnitude, and higher. A hectamagnitude would equal the number "googol", 10^{100}, and would cover a number like 10^{90}. The primary structure of a modest-sized protein, as discussed above, would contain several hectamagnitudes of possible arrangements. Incidentally, a googol (a hectamagnitude) is thought to be a trillion times bigger than the number of elementary particles in the observable universe (Poundstone 1985 p. 94).

Take a million-pixel video screen in which each pixel may glow in one of ten colours. The number of possible configurations of such a screen (consisting of a $1,000 \times 1,000$ matrix) is equal to $10^{1,000,000}$ or to use a double exponent, 10^{10^6}. This would correspond to a megamagnitude but is infinitesimal compared to the number "googolplex" which is a 10 multiplied by itself googol times, ie, $10^{10^{100}}$ (Poundstone 1985 p. 95). Using the terminology described above, a googolplex would be called a googolmagnitude. Information physics will require a specialist set of mathematical terms as it begins to explore advanced information systems.

The Evolution of the Universe

The very large numbers associated with the improbability of advanced information systems causes one to wonder how such systems are possible in the first place. The answer lies in the recursive properties of information systems. Organised systems exhibit resonances. Resonances lead to oscillations. Oscillations represent timed cycles during which changes may be introduced. Such changes may dampen or amplify the existing oscillations. Alternatively, they may create new resonances and excite new sets of oscillations. The more complex the system, the greater the likelihood of introducing changes into the system during any given cycle. Hence the exponential growth of information.

In the light of the preceding considerations it becomes clear that fig. 3.2 which plots the relationship between information and entropy, also plots the evolution of the universe: At the far right – where entropy approaches the infinite, and information the zero state – we have the Big Bang. As we move to the left, the information content of the universe begins to increase, first as the forces of nature – gravity, weak and strong nuclear forces, electromagnetism – differentiate out, then as matter appears. As we move further to the left, we see the evolution of matter into increasingly complex forms. By the time we approach the ordinate – the zero entropy state – self-organising systems begin to appear, and as we move into the left quadrant we see not only the further development of more advanced self-organising systems, we have now reached the realm of biological systems. We also see the emergence of an entirely new phenomenon – intelligence. From here on in, the curve depicting the growth of information becomes increasingly steeper, reflecting the autocatalytic processes which characterise advanced systems capable not only of organising themselves, but, with increasing efficiency, also of ordering their environment.

Viewing the universe as "a recursively defined geometric object" (Poundstone 1985 p. 231), means that complexity builds on complexity. It took of the order of a billion years to evolve from *advanced* single-celled organisms to human beings. It had taken the previous billion years to evolve the "eukaryotic" cell. Such a cell contains a nucleus, mitochondria and a variety of other cell organelles – all linked into a synchronised whole. At least some, and possibly all of these organelles at some previous age, represented independent functioning units, as did the "prokaryotic" cells lacking nuclei. Multicellular organisms arose by linking cells into coherent functioning units. Those made up of prokaryotic cells could link only weakly and created only the most simple of structures such as chains, filaments, and clumps, as today do bacteria and blue-green algae. For advanced, complex multicellular organisms the eukaryotic cell was a prerequisite. The complexity of eukaryotic cells allowed for the diversity needed to allow differentiation into a wide range of cell types, and to permit the development of mechanisms for cell migration and attachment.

To evolve in the first place, eukaryotic cells required the previous existence of prokaryotic cells and other primitive life forms. Early, archaic life forms depended on the prior existence of complex molecules, derived from combinations of simpler molecules, which arose from the forces linking up atoms, which in turn were formed by the intra-atomic forces linking fundamental particles into nucleons and atoms. Complexity utilises pre-existing complexity to achieve higher degrees of complexity, building up the information content of evolving systems *ad infinitum*. It began with the zero information state of the Big

Bang: First the fundamental forces, then matter differentiated; the process of evolution had begun. The exponential growth of information was inevitable.

Improbability fed further on existing improbability. One does not start with zero information and have proverbial monkeys typing at random hoping to author "Hamlet" (Bennet 1977). Instead, a highly advanced information system named William Shakespeare was born into an advanced information culture, and in due course added further information as the universe cycled on.

The concept that as the universe evolves, its information content increases, is in opposition to the idea that the increase in entropy will, inevitably lead to the "heat death" of the universe. However, it reflects the current rethink in physics as reviewed by Paul Davies (1987) in his book *The Cosmic Blueprint* [p. 20]: "There exists alongside the entropy arrow another arrow of time, equally fundamental, and no less subtle in nature ... the universe is *progressing* – through the steady growth of structure, organization and complexity – to ever more developed and elaborate states of matter and energy."

Literature Cited

S Beer (1972) *Brain of the Firm*, Allen Lane/Penguin, London.

WR Bennet (1977) How artificial is intelligence? *Am. Sci.* 65:694–702.

L Brillouin (1956) *Science Information Theory*, Academic Press, New York.

SG Brush (1983) *Statistical Physics and the Atomic Theory of Matter*, Princeton University Press.

C Cherry (1978) *On Human Communication* 3rd edn, The MIT Press, Cambridge, Mass.

P Davies (1987) *The Cosmic Blueprint*, Heinemann, London.

W Greiner and H Stocker (1985) Hot nuclear matter, *Sci. Am.* 252(1):58–66.

RVL Hartley (1928) Transmission of information, *Bell Syst. Tech. J.* 7:535.

W Poundstone (1985) *The Recursive Universe*, Contemporary Books, Chicago.

CE Shannon (1948) A mathematical theory of communication, *Bell Syst. Tech. J.* 27:379,623.

CE Shannon and W Weaver (1964) *The Mathematical Theory of Communication*, University of Illinois Press, Urbana.

A Szent-Gyorgyi (1968) *Bioelectronics*, Academic Press, New York.

L Szilard (1929) Über die Entropieverminderung in einem thermodynamischen System bei Eingriffen intelligenter Wesen, *Z. Physik.* 53:840–856.

J Wicken (1987) Entropy and information: suggestions for a common language, *Philos. Sci.* 54:176–193.

DJ Wineland, JC Bergquist, WM Itano, JJ Bollinger and CH Manney (1987) Atomic-ion coulomb clusters in an ion trap, *Phys. Rev. Lett.* 59(26):2935–2938.

· 6 ·

Some Further Considerations About the Interrelationship Between Information and Energy

Introduction

Energy and information are readily interconvertible. As we have discussed in detail in previous chapters, *entropy*, which in some text books is defined as "bound" energy or energy unavailable for the performance of work, is in reality a measure of the changes in information. If the conclusion at the end of chapter 4 proves correct, then the information changes accompanying altered physical states imply that one joule per degree (K) is equivalent to of the order of 10^{23} bits.

The present chapter explores additional relationships between information and energy. It begins with the consideration that pure energy added to matter results in heat, and that heat is the antithesis of structure. In contrast to heat, all other forms of energy involve organised patterns and may be said to contain information, in the same way that organised matter may be said to contain information. The chapter goes on to explore the phenomenon of motion and its matrix, space and time. Such exploration leads to a reinterpretation of potential energy as a form of information. Finally, the chapter considers the work of information machines. In the interaction between matter, energy and information, two types of information are clearly discernible: structural information, and kinetic information. The latter is equated to potential energy.

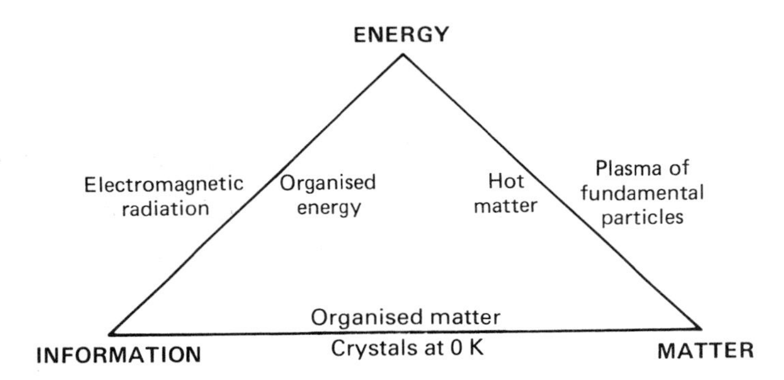

Fig. 6.1

Pure Energy: Heat, the Antithesis of Information

Heat constitutes pure energy interacting with matter.* The application of heat, by itself, constitutes no input of information. An increase in heat causes molecules or other particles to move more randomly. It causes a crystal to melt – then vaporises a liquid into gas. At each stage, the system becomes less organised. The application of heat to a system brings about a randomisation of its components – it produces disorder in the universe. The converse, withdrawing heat from a system such as condensing a gas, or freezing a liquid, brings about an increase in organisation. Such cooling processes therefore are associated with an increase in information.

***Heat* is the product of *energy* interacting with matter. *Structure* represents the product of *information* interacting with matter.**

The application of energy expresses itself as heat which causes particles (molecules, phonons, plasmons, etc) to vibrate and to move at random. In contrast, the application of information causes particles to be bound into fixed patterns and ordered motion. In that sense, heat may be considered as the antithesis of organisation.

If heat is the antithesis of organisation, and, by implication,

---

* The term "heat" as used in the present context is equivalent to uncorrelated phonons in a crystal or the random motion of molecules in a gas. It must not be confused with, for example, energy radiated as infra-red radiation.

energy the antithesis of information, that does not preclude the possibility that energy and information may interact to provide a mix which might be viewed as "energised information", or alternatively as "structured energy". INFORMATION and ENERGY must not be viewed as the opposites of a bipolar system, rather, they must be considered as the two angles of a triangle, with MATTER comprising the third.

Such a conceptual model would define the boundaries of our physical universe: The three sides of the triangle – the extremes – in terms of the following phenomena (see fig. 6.1):

(1) A mixture of pure energy and matter, lacking information, would comprise a plasma of fundamental particles. (2) A mixture of matter and pure information, lacking energy, would be exemplified by a crystal at 0 K. (3) A mixture of information and energy, lacking matter, would consist of massless particles such as photons travelling through space devoid of matter.

The Information Content of Energy

Consider a radio wave. Obviously, as a form of electromagnetic radiation, it represents a form of energy. However, a radio wave carries a lot of information. Not only the human information superimposed on the carrier wave to reproduce the human voice or music, but the carrier wave itself: The carrier wave has a basic frequency which reflects the resonance of the transmitting circuit. Such a resonance, in turn, is a function of the structure, both electronic and physical, that is, of the information content of the system. Thus even an unmodulated radio wave carries the information imparted to it by the resonance of the transmitter.

In fact, all forms of energy other than heat, contain an information component: Mechanical energy involves motion, which, as we shall discuss in greater detail below, involves distance, time and direction, all three of which represent forms of information. Sound energy is dependent on the organisation of the medium which propagates it. Chemical energy is dependent on the patterns of electronic structures of the atoms and molecules involved as reactants. Osmotic work depends on the organisation of semi-permeable membranes. Electrical energy is dependent on structures which allow non-random charges to build up. Atomic energy relates to the organisation of the atomic nucleus. Thus, *all forms of energy other than heat exhibit, or are dependent upon some sort of organisation or pattern in respect to space or time*. Only heat involves complete randomness, both in space and time.

The idea that different forms of energy may contain different amounts of information and represent a mixture of pure energy plus information, may seem strange at first: Energy is energy, and one form may be readily converted into another: Not only is there a great body of experimental and practical experience, but theory has established the precise formulae for describing (and predicting) such interconversions.

Nevertheless, engineers have traditionally considered that heat constitutes a form of low grade energy while mechanical energy is a higher form. It is time to scrap these imprecise terms and instead analyse the various forms of energy in terms of their information content. Surely it makes intuitive sense that a beam of coherent light contains more information than a beam of incoherent light of equal energy content. What intuition perceives is the existence of a pattern. A beam of coherent light has its waves moving in phase, while the waves of incoherent light move at random. However, as alluded to above, even incoherent light has a pattern: Each photon has a distinct frequency and a constancy of speed.

Ice, liquid water, and steam represent matter whose form is determined by the amount of energy contained within it. We can measure temperature and are able to predict when we have added enough energy to convert ice to water, or water to steam. In a similar manner, the various forms of *energy* reflect the nature and amount of information contained within them. We need to devise instruments which are able to measure precisely the information content of various forms of energy.

Motion, Distance and Time

Motion is implicitly intertwined with information: All motion involves a reorganisation of the universe. The act of moving any entity from one place to another must comprise an information act. In chapter 2, we emphasised that one must not confuse the three interrelated phenomena of *force*, *momentum* and *motion*, the first two representing aspects of energy, while the last represents a form of information. Lastly, we considered that since Galileo's classic experiments, physicists and engineers have described all motion in terms of distance, time and direction.

Changes in distance per unit time, measure the changes in the information content of the system containing the moving particle. Specifically, they measure the particle in relation to some frame of reference, and how this relation changes.

Space and time are organisational properties of the universe. Proof of this assertion is the general exclusion principle which states that no two solids may occupy the same space at the same time. As will be discussed in the appendixes, Pauli's exclusion principle applied to the orbiting electrons of an atom, could also be interpreted this way except that instead of dealing with the organisation of material, one is dealing with the organisation of "energetic" space within atomic shells.

Space may be measured by distance. We also know how to carve it up in abstract ways – intersecting planes, geometric objects, both two and three dimensional – our primate heritage coupled to our advanced brain has allowed us to play with space – Euclidian geometry, Riemanian geometry, topology ...

Time is much fuzzier. The perception and analysis of time was not as important to our primate ancestors as was the perception and analysis of space. In earlier cultures, if time was considered at all, it was diffuse and cyclic. Western thought made it linear, uni-directional and divisible. The matter has been admirably analysed and reviewed by Geza Szamosi (1986a, 1986b):

It was Galileo who first clearly established that time is the independent variable in the description of motion. Using a water clock, he was the first to time physical events, establishing that all the important features of motion – distance moved, velocity, and acceleration – all were a function of time.

Besides allowing Galileo to formulate the laws of falling bodies, his experiments led to a new conceptual view of the world. This new perception of time was codified by Newton about half a century later: "Absolute, true, and mathematical time, of itself, and from its own nature, flows equably without relation to anything external." As Szamosi points out, time came to be seen as an absolute, independent dimension which could be used to measure motion. This contrasts with the earlier Platonic view that time was a product of motion, particularly the motion of the sun and planets, a view reinforced by Aristotle who attributed time to the motion of any object and emphasised its everlasting cyclic nature.

Part of the problem is that the word "time", in our culture, means several things, not one. Unlike space, where we understand the abstract concept "space", and do not confuse it with measurements of space (ie, "distance"), "time" serves both the abstract concept and the measurement of it. In fact, the term "time" is used to refer to a number of distinct, although interrelated concepts: It may refer to a dimension of indefinite, continuous duration (the absolute time of Newton), while at the same time it may also be used to describe a less definite portion (eg, a historical period), or a definite portion (eg, a season), or a fixed point in time, as when two people meet at a specific hour.

We know how to deal with space, but time remains an elusive entity. As G.J. Whitrow (1975) has pointed out, "time has this peculiar quality which makes us feel intuitively that we understand it perfectly so long as we are not asked to explain what we mean by it" [p. 11].

In the present work we will define space as the interval between matter, and time as the interval between events. Both space and time can be measured by means of human artefacts such as a ruler or a chronometer. Once such artefacts exist, one can divide up space and time in a purely abstract manner. That is, one can invent abstract points in space and, using a ruler, measure abstract space – even if our imaginary point is in the middle of an absolute vacuum, lacking all matter. In a similar manner, one can invent an event, set the clock to it, and measure the time interval from there on.

Measurements of space and time establish information about the distribution and organisation of matter and energy.

Space measurements (ie, distances) are related to matter. One needs fixed points as landmarks to measure distances: the distance between two cities, the distance from earth to sun, the time it takes light to travel between two points. Just as it becomes virtually impossible to judge distances without reference points in the middle of the ocean, so does it become impossible in a vacuum – we cannot measure space until we introduce a frame of reference. Introduce two molecules, and we can now talk of the "empty space" between them. We can define this (empty) space in terms of the distance between the two molecules. Similarly with time: Envisage a vacuum, totally black, devoid of all energy. Now introduce a pulse of light.

Then a second pulse. The interval between the two pulses might be described as "empty time" – nothing happening. We can define this (empty) time as the interval between the two pulses of light.

An organised system occupies space and time. The amount of space occupied can be measured in units of distance. Other things being equal, the larger a (non-empty) system, the more information it contains because either it contains more units, or the same number of units are regulated at greater distances by more powerful linkages. In the physical world, if a system expands in space as a result of the application of energy, there is no change in information unless there is also a change in organisation: If the applied energy causes an increase in entropy, and the expanding system becomes more random (as with a gas being heated), then the system loses information. However, if the system retains its organisation as it expands, then the linkages between the units must be relatively more powerful to be able to operate at greater distances – the expanded system (retaining its structure) is thermodynamically more improbable than its original version.

For example, it takes more energy, and more organisation in the nucleus of the atom to maintain electrons in an outer shell, ie, at a greater distance from the centre. The heavier elements in the periodic table not only contain more information units (nucleons and electrons), and show more differentiation and organisation, but they also occupy more space.

As a rule, therefore, *the information content of a system is directly proportional to the space it occupies*.

The opposite holds true for time. Time, like entropy, is inversely related to information. The greater the interval

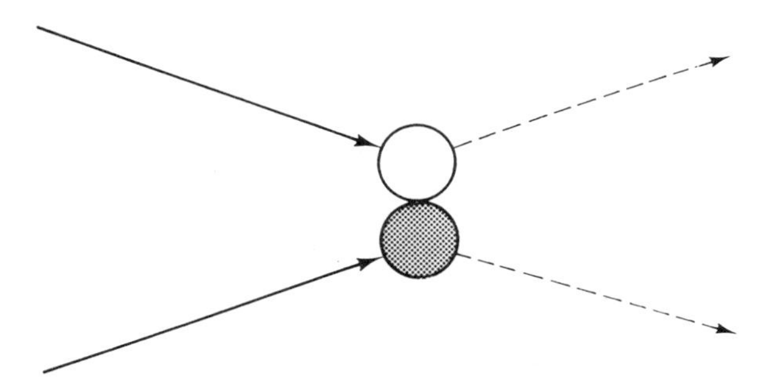

Fig. 6.2

between two events, the less the information content of the system.

The idea that an increase in time between events implies that the system has less information, should not be confused with the structural information content of a system which persists longer in time. Obviously, a system which survives the "ravages of time" is likely to contain more information than one which disintegrates. However, the same may be said for entropy: A system which survives the "forces of entropy" is likely to contain more information (such as a system possessing homeostatic mechanisms) than one which becomes rapidly disorganised. Therefore, one must not confuse the information content of a system able to withstand the ravages of time (or the forces of entropy) with time (or entropy) itself. Time (like entropy) is inversely related to information: The longer the interval between two events, the fewer events per unit time, and the less information is contained by the system.

We shall shortly examine further the interconversion of energy and information. Suffice it to say here that the greater the energy content of a system, the greater the potential information content of the system (if it can be made to perform "useful" work). The energy content of two bodies of equal mass in motion may be ascertained by their respective velocities. This does not hold for photons, whose rest mass is zero. Whether one measures acceleration, or constant speed, in all cases, time is inversely related to the energy of the moving body: The more time it takes for a moving body to traverse a certain distance, the less its energy, the less its capacity to perform work, and, by implication, the less its potential information.

In general, therefore, other things being equal, the information content of a system tends to vary directly with the space it occupies and inversely with the time it occupies.

G.J. Whitrow [pp. 140–141] has reviewed the idea that neither time nor space may be infinitely divisible – rather that, like matter and energy, they may be atomic or particulate in fine structure. According to such a speculation, the minimum spatial displacement may be about 10^{-12} mm, corresponding to the effective diameter of an electron. The corresponding minimum time – the *chronon* – would be the time required for light to cross such a distance (10^{-24} s). Only time will tell if such a concept will prove to reflect physical reality.

The organisation of matter and energy in space and time comprises information. If we remove matter and energy, we would be left with empty space, and empty time. Would there still exist information? We will discuss this matter later. What should become clear, however, is that the measurement of abstract distance and time constitutes information. And so does the measurement of changes in respect to distance and time. This is why all bodies in motion must be considered to contain information, information imparted by the force which initiated the trajectory of the moving body.

Such consideration leads to a reinterpretation of well-known physical phenomena: For example, consider two billiard balls, one red, one white, rolling along on a billiard table at equal speed. The red one is moving in a north-easterly direction, while the white one is moving in a south-easterly direction. Let them meet in such a way, that the collision results in a reversal of direction: The red one now travelling south-east, while the white one travels north-east (see fig. 6.2).

The question that one may ask is whether the two balls exchanged *energy*, or whether they exchanged *information*. Certainly the collision, involving a glancing blow, seemed not to affect appreciably the energy content of the system as a whole. Nor did the energy content of the individual balls appear to be affected appreciably since they continued moving at virtually undiminished speed. What was altered however, was the direction: The red ball, instead of heading for the north-east corner, ended up in the south-east, while the converse was true for the white ball. To restate the question: Is the conservation of momentum a reflection of the fact that the two bodies merely exchanged information?

Information and Potential Energy

When I pick up a pencil off the floor and place it on my desk I have created a quantity called "potential energy". That is, the pencil, lying innocently on my desk, has become imbued with this magical quantity, potential energy. The fact that the pencil will not move until exposed to another force, is ignored. The pencil now contains bottled up energy which will express itself only if somehow the pencil is pushed, or rolls off the desk.

In truth, the pencil will not move until someone or something applies another force to it.

How much more intuitive would be the interpretation that when I picked up the pencil, I engaged in an act of mechanical work which changed the organisation of the universe. That is, the output of mechanical work resulted in a change in the information status of the system being worked upon.

Let us consider another example: The fate of a ball thrown up into the air. As it rises it slows down, then at its peak, as the force of the throw and the force of gravity balance each other, it remains suspended in mid air before starting its descent. This observation has always posed a problem as to what has happened to the energy when a ball passes through its stationary phase in mid air. Traditionally, the answer has been to postulate two kinds of energy: kinetic and potential. Kinetic energy relates to motion, and potential energy relates to position or configuration. Thus the rising ball converts kinetic energy into potential energy, until finally, at the apex its kinetic energy is zero while its potential energy is maximum. Upon its descent, the reverse process takes place, so that by the time it hits the earth, kinetic energy is at a maximum and the potential energy is now zero.

If the ball is made of rubber, or some other compressible material, and if the ground consists of a hard surface such as a concrete court, the ball bounces. Again, momentarily the ball remains stationary on the ground before flying upward again. At this point its kinetic energy is once again zero, while its potential energy suddenly has increased dramatically as a result of the ball's change in shape. As the ball returns to its original spherical shape, the ball accelerates rapidly and regains kinetic, while it loses potential, energy. As the ball bounces back upward – as it leaves the ground – the ball once again possesses high kinetic and low potential energy.

Note that this explanation of an everyday phenomenon not only needs to involve two different kinds of energy, kinetic and potential, but two different kinds of potential energy: The energy which suspends the ball in mid air, *gravitational potential energy*; and the potential energy which causes the ball to bounce back, *configurational potential energy*.

The same phenomenon analysed by the information physicist would scrap the term "potential energy", and substitute the term "information". Keeping in mind that one characteristic of information is its thermodynamic improbability, both the ball suspended in mid air, and the ball in a highly distorted, compressed state, represent highly improbable states. A ball propelled upwards transforms energy into information until at the moment it reaches its peak, all the energy supplied by the ball thrower has been momentarily transformed into pure information. Theoretically, if the ball were propelled with sufficient force (and at the correct angle), it could end up in a geostationary orbit: The ball instead of rotating around the earth's axis (while lying on the ground), now rotates at a much greater distance (out in space). Under those circumstances, energy would have been applied, and work would have been performed, to change the organisation of the system.

We need not place the ball in geostationary orbit, we need only pick the ball off the ground and place it on the table. In this case, we have applied energy to perform work, and the work has resulted in a change in the organisation of the system. To say that all the energy used in moving the ball from the floor to the table, is now energy bottled up in the form of potential energy is shirking the fact that the ball is at rest (let us put it in a bowl for safe-keeping) and will not move again until a new force is applied to it. The energy which the ball contained while it was moving (its kinetic energy) has disappeared. There will be no further change until another force is applied. For practical purposes there is no more energy. As with the pencil replaced on the desk, it would be much more logical to consider that when the ball was picked up off the floor and put in the bowl, work was performed to change the information content of the system. For this reason we may consider as axiomatic the following definition of potential energy:

Potential energy is a term which describes a process in which the expenditure of energy has brought about a change in the organisational state of a system such that its information content has increased.

Both the term "bound energy" used to describe entropy, and the term "potential energy", represent the accounting devices of traditional physics used to explain the apparent disappearance of a quantity of energy. In both instances one is dealing with the interconversion of energy and information. Such conversions may be permanent or transient. We shall discuss shortly the quantitative relationships between work and information, and the direct, linear relation between potential energy and information.

The Interconversion of Energy and Information

Traditional physics, in this century, learned to accept the idea that energy may be converted into matter. For example, under certain circumstances a high energy photon may be converted into an electron and a positron. Information physics considers that energy may also be converted into information. This occurs under circumstances in which a system exhibits either a decrease in entropy, or an increase in potential energy.

The "Bénard instability" represents such an example: It appears under certain circumstances when the lower surface of a horizontal liquid layer is heated (as reviewed by Prigogine and Stengers 1985). A vertical temperature gradient sets up a permanent heat flux moving from bottom to top. If the gradient is not too great, the heat is conveyed by conduction alone. However, as the heat applied increases (slowly), a threshold value is reached in which convection becomes important in transferring heat from the lower to the upper surface. In the Bénard instability, this process may involve a highly organised movement of molecules. As Prigogine and Stengers describe it [p. 142]: "The Bénard instability is a spectacular phenomenon ... Millions of molecules move coherently, forming hexagonal convection cells of a characteristic size." Instead of producing a mere increase in disorganisation with the further application of heat, the Bénard instability creates structures which aid the transfer of heat across the layer of liquid. The authors also make the important point [p. 143] that: "heat transfer was considered a sort of waste in classical thermodynamics. In the Bénard cell it becomes a source of order".

Here, then, is a clear case where the application of energy, results in increasing the organisation of the system. This particular form of organisation is maintained only as long as there is a heat flux of sufficient magnitude across the horizontal layer of liquid. Once the energy is withdrawn, the structure collapses – the information disappears. (Of course, if the input of heat is too great, then the liquid can no longer transport the heat fast enough to the upper, cooler surface, and the convection currents become increasingly turbulent as the liquid begins to boil.)

Information Machines

A radio transmitter emitting radio waves carrying human information is an example of an information machine. Both the frequency of the carrier, and its modulation, involve imposing patterns of information on "raw" energy. For a radio transmitter, the "raw energy" consists of an input of electrical energy. In order to obtain electricity one needs a generator, which may consist of a steam turbine. Such a steam turbine starts with pure energy in the form of heat to create steam, the steam then may drive a piston or a turbine to convert heat energy into mechanical energy, which then drives a generator to convert the mechanical into electric energy. The electric energy is converted by the radio transmitter into electromagnetic radiation, which in turn, is modulated further to carry human messages. At each step, the energy becomes more organised as it is processed by human information machines. We start with coal heating steam, and end up with a voice speaking through our radio's loudspeaker.

Obviously, human information machines are able to impose patterns of information on various forms of energy. However, they are able to accomplish two other tasks as well: First, as is well known, they act as energy transducers, able to convert one form of energy into another. Second, under certain circumstances they convert energy into information, and vice versa.

Take the example of radio transmission. A single radio announcer with a single microphone may reach a million homes. The information has been multiplied a million-fold. (It is irrelevant that the human information content is identical in each case – the physical information has been multiplied a million times.) This huge increase in the quantity of physical information must have come from somewhere.

A similar argument can be made for the output of other human information machines such as printing presses or computers. In fact, our human environment is filled with devices which either convert energy into information, or use energy to convert information from one form to another (information transducers). Devices which convert energy into information include electronic signal generators, radios, printing presses, traffic signals, computers, clocks.

Take an electric clock. It converts electrical energy into mechanical energy via an electric motor. The electric motor pushes the hands of the clock (or it may move digits if it is a mechanical, digital clock). A traditional analysis would consider the work output to consist of (force × distance) moving the hands of the clock. A side product would be heat, and the entropy of the universe would have been increased. Yet the clock also provides information. It may be used as a timer to turn on a video recorder, turn off a microwave oven, or operate delicate machinery in a factory. More subtle is the fact that reasonably accurate time devices are crucial for the coordination of modern society. The clock in a railway station may determine the departure time of trains. The output of a station clock may therefore decrease the entropy in the universe by organising a tansportation network. If we knew how to quantify these links, we might discover the precise relationship between the work output of a clock and its output of information.

A computer is the most obvious example of a human information machine. It is a device specifically dedicated to the task of processing information. When it generates a letter on a visual display unit, each character space responsible for generating a letter is the same – comprised of similar grids of pixels (the simplest usually consisting of a 5 × 8 grid), with the pixel as the basic unit of information. Which letter is displayed is determined by the pattern of the pixels. Theoretically, pixels which are "on", and pixels which are "off", both contain equivalent information. There is no difference in the information content of a "0" or a "1" position of the binary switch. The significance of the position of each switch is determined by the pattern of on/off switches or pixels. It is the ability to create patterns, which is inherent in information machines.

One could analyse the work performed by a computer purely in terms of the electron beam generated in the cathode ray tube and the consequent light and heat emitted by the screen. However, that is like analysing the intellectual output of an Einstein in terms of the breakfast he ate. Both Einstein and the computer converted a certain portion of the energy inputs into information outputs.

Not only computers, but all machines contain information. Spinning wheels and power looms contain within them an accumulation of experience and inventions – a whole history of information inputs. The information contained within the spinning wheel, when coupled to further inputs of matter and energy in the form of fleece and a human spinner, helps to organise matter further by creating patterns, ie, by converting fleece to yarn. In a similar manner, a power loom converts yarn into cloth. For the raw material (fleece, yarn), *machines* (spinning wheels, looms) *comprise part of an ordered environment which can create further order*. Thus machinery not only contains information, but part of the work performed by machines involves the creation of new information.

All machinery contains stored information. In general, machinery contributes to a further ordering of the universe. This is as true for non-human machinery as it is for human inventions. The metabolic machinery of a single cell, when having successfully completed its various processes, will have produced another cell. The enzymes and membranes of that cell will have catalysed chemical reactions by providing an ordered environment for these reactions to take place. In the absence of such an information-rich environment, some of the reactions might have taken a hundred years to complete. The cell would have died long before then.

Living systems, which include the human brain, possess the most complex information machinery known. However, inorganic systems, such as a crystal template favouring the growth of that crystal may also be considered in terms of an information machine. The theory of cellular automata in artificial intelligence has led some theorists (eg, Poundstone 1985 p. 231) to suggest that the entire universe should be viewed as "a recursively defined geometric object". Such a concept may easily be extended to consider the universe as a gigantic information machine processing matter, energy, and information.

Structural vs Kinetic Information

In analysing the work performed by a steam engine, one must differentiate clearly between the *inherent* information which comprises a part of the engine, and the information *applied* by the engine. The former owes its existence to people like Boyle, Newcomen, Watt, and all the other scientists, engineers and artisans who provided the information needed for the design of a successful engine. The latter, the *information applied*, is that which creates the non-equilibrium situation and couples it to a countervailing force so as to produce work. The former, the inherent information, is the information contained by organised structures and may therefore be also called *structural information*. The latter, the applied information, is information in action, and may be considered as *kinetic information*.

If we envisage a hypothetical demon (Maxwell's demon) sorting out the swifter molecules from the slower ones in a chamber of gas, the demon itself would possess "structural" information. The product of the demon's work – the separation of the two types of molecules – would result in a disequilibrium situation. Such a situation would, in traditional physics, be called "potential energy". Information physics would class it as "kinetic information".

The expression "potential energy", in fact, covers two classes of information: structural and kinetic. If the reorganisation of the universe ends up in a "stable" equilibrium situation, such as a pencil placed on a desk, or a ball placed in a bowl on a table, then the energy of the work process has been converted into *structural* information. If on the other hand, the reorganisation is in an "unstable" state, far from equilibrium, and about to change, then one is dealing with *kinetic* information. A ball thrown up into the air at its apogee, a bouncing ball compressed on the ground, the compressed steam in a running steam engine – all these are examples of kinetic information – information about to be reconverted to energy.

Entropy is sometimes considered as a form of "bound energy" which cannot be used to perform work (eg, Schafroth 1960). In order to produce work, part of the energy supplied must be in the form of, or converted to, kinetic information. Such information represents the thermodynamic improbability of the disequilibrium situation which all energy transducers must create in order to produce useful work (see chapter 7). It is that fraction of energy converted to kinetic information which becomes lost as the information becomes degraded to heat during the process of work, which comprises this bound (unavailable) energy, responsible for the observed increase in entropy.

In a process producing work, therefore, the kinetic information *used up* reflects the difference between the entropy of the state at the beginning of the work process when it is at maximum disequilibrium (S_1), and the entropy of the system at the end of the work process, when it has achieved equilibrium (S_2).

The kinetic information *added* by an energy transducer is reflected by the difference in entropy contained by the system originally (S_0) and after the disequilibrium situation has been achieved (S_1).

It would seem reasonable to suppose that, in general, the ability of an energy transducer to supply *kinetic* information is a function of its *structural* information. An organised system is able to accomplish work at temperatures T, at which unorganised systems could not. We will discuss in the next chapter the example of the photosynthetic system of a plant cell which is able to dissociate water and strip electrons off hydrogen atoms at 25°C. In a simple (less information rich) physical system, such a process requires temperatures exceeding 1,000°C. Therefore, intuitively one would argue that the ability of an energy transducer to generate a large quantity of kinetic information, must be a function of the structural information contained within it. A high pressure steam engine should contain more structural information than a low pressure engine.

However, consider two steam engines of identical make and design. Both are equally efficient in producing work, but one is used on a fairground and has been elaborately decorated. The decorated engine therefore would possess more structural information yet be no more efficient.

A less trivial example is provided by isozymes. Isozymes are enzymes which perform identical biochemical functions, but whose structures differ. One such class of enzymes, shown to consist of dozens of isozymes, are the peroxidases. These protein catalysts regulate a number of reactions involved with the oxidation or reduction of a wide variety of compounds. Some of these reactions are highly specific: The active sites on the various isozymes are the same. However, other parts of the protein may be quite different. One reason for this difference is that the other parts of the protein molecule are responsible for attaching the enzymes to some cell structure such as a cell wall or a membrane system, or alternatively, keeping the enzyme soluble.

If some of the structure of the protein relates to its location inside a cell, other structural information relates to its own maintenance. That is, the molecule must be stable and maintain its integrity in a complex (sometimes hostile) environment. Consider, for example, the disulphide linkages across chains of polypeptides, so important in determining the tertiary structure of a protein (see chapter 4) – at least some of these are likely to function in the maintenance of the shape of the molecule.

Obviously not all of the structural information contained in an enzyme is directly related to its catalytic function.

Part of the structural information of a steam engine relates to its location. Is it on wheels because it functions as a locomotive? Is it in the hold of a steam ship? Or does it stand on a factory floor? Likewise, some of its structural information relates to protecting it from environmental vicissitude. In analysing the structural information of energy transducers, therefore, one must differentiate between structural information which is directly relevant to the production of kinetic information, and that which is not. In the case of an enzyme, the active site (where the electronic structures of the reactants are reorganised) obviously is relevant while the part which attaches the enzyme to the cell membrane probably is not. Similarly, the cylinder and piston of a steam engine is relevant, while the bolts which fix it to the factory floor, are not.

Unfortunately, the matter is more complex. If the steam engine were not bolted to the floor, it would rattle around and bend the drive shaft mechanism, if not blow up. And the precise location of an enzyme in a cell, often coupled to other nearby enzymes, may be crucial to its function. To define precisely the relationship between the structural information contained within an energy transducer, and the kinetic information provided by such a device, constitutes one of the major problems confronting the field of information physics. Any such analyses must be able to operate at a minimum of two organisational levels: (1) At the *individual* reaction, or process level, analysing the kinetic information produced to foster an individual chemical reaction, or the output of a single steam engine. (2) At the *systems* level in which the individual enzyme is put into the context of a battery of enzymes or the metabolic machinery of a cell, and a power lathe as one of a series of machines in a factory carefully positioned to facilitate assembly line production.

Transformations Between Kinetic and Structural Information

Kinetic and structural information must also be interconvertible. Kinetic information can remain kinetic only as long as the system is in a state of disequilibrium. As soon as the system reaches equilibrium, ie, becomes static, the kinetic information will have disappeared: Either it will have been degraded into heat, having first been reconverted to kinetic energy; or alternatively, the performance of work has resulted in a reorganisation of the universe so as to produce new structural information.

The ball tossed into the air contained kinetic information until it returned to the ground. Suppose the ball had ended up in geostationary orbit, or alternatively, merely in the gutter of a nearby roof. It would remain wedged there until dislodged by another force. The ball in the gutter would be in a stable, equilibrium situation. If not as useful to humans as the walls and the roof of the house, the ball would be as stable and as much a part of the structure as the bricks piled upon each other making up the wall, or the tiles of the roof where the ball was wedged. The kinetic information of the ball, therefore, was transformed into structural information. Similarly, what applies to a ball being moved from ground level to some higher state, applies to other systems as well, as, for example the shift of an electron to an outer shell in an atom as a result of absorbing a photon. Actually, the preceding statements are incorrect. Strictly speaking, the information content of either the ball itself, or of the electron, has *not* changed. What has changed is the information content of the *systems* which contain the moving bodies: Moving an electron to an outer shell does not mean that the electron itself has undergone a change in information status. However, the atom has. It is now in a thermodynamically more improbable state – the atom, not the electron, has gained information.

There is another problem: If the ball lodged on the roof is tightly wedged into a crevice, does the system possess the *same* amount of structural information as when the ball is precariously balanced on a ledge? Intuitively, one would say that in the former state, the system contains more information.

Such an intuition would be incorrect. Both systems would contain the same amount of information (providing it took the same amount of work to place the balls in their respective position on the roof). However, the system with the ball on the ledge of the roof, is much more likely to lose the information.

One might quantify such a situation by measuring the "activation energy", ie, the amount of work required to dislodge the ball so as to, once more, convert the structural information of the system into kinetic information (the ball about to fall). Once the ball had been dislodged, the kinetic information would then be transformed into kinetic energy as the ball begins its descent.

The ball-on-the-roof system may represent a trivial example. However, it does illustrate a fundamental principle : *The greater the activation energy required to destroy the structural information contained by a system, the greater are its chances of survival.* The negative entropy represented by biological systems is the product of forces selecting increasingly survivable information systems. New information is often added for the sole purpose of stabilising and preserving existing information structures. This is true not only for biological systems, but also for human societal, technological, and linguistic systems.

The accumulation of information to create increasingly improbable structures and systems, that is the increase in negative entropy, involves *information work*. **Information work involves work in which part of the energy applied ends up as an increase in information.**

Literature Cited

W Poundstone (1985) *The Recursive Universe*, Contemporary Books, Chicago.
I Prigogine and I Stengers (1985) *Order Out of Chaos*, Flamingo/Fontana Paperbacks, London.
MR Schafroth (1960) The concept of temperature, *Selected Lectures in Modern Physics*, Macmillan, London.
G Szamosi (1986a) The origin of time, *The Sciences*, New York Acad. Sci. Sept/Oct 1986, pp. 33–39.
G Szamosi (1986b) *The Twin Dimensions – Inventing Time and Space*, McGraw-Hill, New York.
GJ Whitrow (1975) *The Nature of Time*, Penguin Books, Harmondsworth.

· 7 ·

Information and Work

Introduction

"Work" is a transient phenomenon – it is a process. Work cannot be stored as such. However, the *product* of work may be stored as a change in the energy content of the system acted upon. In addition, in line with the previous discussion, the product of work may also be stored as a change in *organisation*: When (as discussed in the preceding chapter) I pick up a pencil from the floor and replace it on the desk from which it fell, I am engaging in an act of mechanical work. If that act of work is transient, the new position of the pencil is not. The pencil will remain in its new position until another force acts on it – that is, until more work is applied – thereby changing its *position* once more.

Therefore when I picked up the pencil and placed it on the desk, I changed the organisation of the universe (albeit only a small part of it). Picking up the pencil illustrates the axiom:

The performance of mechnical work causes a change in the organisation of the universe.

Insofar as a change in organisation reflects a change in information, we may state the theorem:

The performance of mechanical work causes a change in the information content of the system acted upon.

The emphasis on "mechanical work" reflects the fact that in classical physics, the term "work" is more general, and may, for example, involve the application of non-specific heat to cause a gas to expand. Therefore, "work", in the classical sense, acting on a system may cause either a change in the information content, or in the energy content of the system, or of both. The performance of non-specific work upon a system is not an automatic measure of the amount of information added to that system. On the other hand, as we will discuss later, in the case of a highly organised form of work, electrical work, the increase in information of the system is directly proportional to the input of work.

The Relationship Between Work and Information

The relationship between work and information is twofold. There is first the relationship discussed above: The performance of work may cause a change in the information content of the system acted upon. The second relationship is the reverse: To obtain "useful" work, a system must be provided not only with energy, but with information as well.

When considering the general term "work", the direction in which bodies move may be random. This is the case for molecules in a gas being heated – the molecules move faster, but at random. In contrast, to obtain useful work, the system must be given further information: In a steam engine, the accelerated molecules of steam, moving at random, bounce off the solid walls of the steam cylinder, but push the head of the piston in a single direction. Thus the energy supplied to the cylinder of a steam engine is converted not only into work by pushing the piston a certain distance with a certain amount of force, but the energy supplied also pushes the piston in a fixed *direction* in accordance with the plans (information input) of the designer. In a steam engine, it is by converting the applied heat energy into both physical force and information, that we are able to produce *useful* work.

"Useful" work is work which increases the organisation of a system. Useless work, in contrast, merely increases the entropy. Useful work, therefore, entails in part, the transformation of energy into information.

As discussed previously, heat constitutes a form of energy which is unorganised. All other forms of energy contain some measure of information, and may thus be considered, at least in part, organised energy.

Therefore, in theory, the application of energy to a system may result in one of four possible changes in the system:

1. The energy is merely absorbed as non-specific heat thereby increasing the entropy.
2. The input of energy causes the system itself to become more highly organised (for example, when a photon is absorbed, an electron is shifted to an outer shell, causing the atom to achieve a more improbable state thermodynamically).
3. The system performs physical (eg, mechanical) work.
4. The system performs information work (eg, by creating an organic polymer).

All four may occur in any combination. All affect the organisation of the system in some manner, hence its information content. In the first case, the system gains energy, but in the process it becomes more disorganised; therefore there is a net loss of information. In the fourth case, the reverse may happen if the formation of the polymer involves an exothermic reaction.

Thus the changes in the content of energy, or information brought about by the application (or withdrawal) of energy to (from) a system, may vary independently. Consider the following cases:

1. When a liquid is evaporated, or ice melts, the energy content increases while the organisation decreases.
2. In an exothermic chemical reaction creating a polymer, the energy content decreases while the organisation increases.
3. In a photosynthesising alga which duplicates itself, the energy and information both increase within the system.

Note that when energy is added (as pure heat, chemical energy, or light), it is not possible for *both* the energy and the information content to decline. Presumably, if either the information or the energy remain constant, then an input of energy causes the other factor to increase. Similarly, if energy is given up by the system, then one or the other must decline – but not necessarily both. For example when water freezes (when heat is given up by the system), the water molecules become more organised; hence, although the energy content of the system decreases, its information content increases. On the other hand, when sugar dissolves in water, giving up heat to the environment, there is a concommitant loss of information as well.

Thus changes in the information and the energy content of a system may vary independently – it is the *nature* of the energy supplied or withdrawn, which will determine the nature of the changes occurring in the system acted upon.

Energy Transducers

To obtain work, one needs to apply energy. To obtain useful work, one needs to apply not only energy, but information as well. Therefore to obtain useful work, the applied energy must either contain information itself, or act on some organised object or device which acts as an "energy transducer" (or both). Such a device may be a fairly "simple" and inert body, such as a dugout canoe with a sail being propelled by the wind (although both the canoe and the sail are highly organised structures containing an enormous amount of information). Or, by contemporary standards, it may be highly complex, such as a nuclear reactor generating high pressure steam. In all cases, energy transducers possess organisation – whether they be an individual atom, a photovoltaic cell, a protein molecule, a membrane, a cell, a battery, a steam engine, a nuclear reactor, or whatever. All exhibit organisation. All possess structural information without which they could not act as energy transducers.

The term energy transducer is used here to describe any system which converts an input of energy into useful work. A black body absorbing light and being heated by it, then reradiating the energy (at a lower level) is not necessarily a transducer. Such a black body performs no useful work but merely transforms the energy from one form to another and increases the entropy of the universe.

Energy transducers create two conditions necessary for the production of useful work: (1) They create a non-equilibrium situation; and (2) they provide a mechanism of countervailing force necessary for the production of useful work.

Three examples will suffice:

A. In the cylinder of a steam engine there is created:
   1. a highly asymmetric distribution of molecules with the highly energetic molecules (as steam) at one end, and the relatively low energetic molecules at the other;

   2. interposed between these two kinds of molecules is a piston which drives a wheel, a pump, or some other mechanical device.

B. A photovoltaic cell:
   1. contains atoms or molecules which absorb photons. The absorbed energy causes electrons to be raised to higher energy levels which leads to unstable configurations;
   2. these instabilities are exploited by trapping electrons into an electrical circuit which can produce work.

C. A living cell may contain an enzyme, which
   1. removes, or adds electrons to the atoms or molecules of the reactant, thereby making it unstable;
   2. this instability is then utilised to couple the reactant to other reactants, or to itself, to form a polymer or other useful product.

An enzyme, simply acting as a catalyst in a chemical system, merely accelerates the displacement of a reaction towards equilibrium. Without further organisation (information), this would merely increase the entropy – it would be a sheer waste of the information contained in the catalyst – a great inefficiency. Therefore, living systems set the stage, so that the reaction activated by the enzyme produces a useful product – thereby accomplishing useful work.

In each of the three examples, the first step involved creating a non-equilibium condition; the second, coupling this disequilibrium to a mechanism which produces useful work. The first step organises the non-equilibrium condition by adding information. This becomes the kinetic information which manifests itself as a decline in entropy from some equilibrium state S_0 to some disequilibrium state with lower entropy S_1. In example A this involved a non-equilibrium distribution of molecules; in B and C it involved the non-equilibrium distribution of electrons in atoms or molecules.

Having created a reduction in entropy by organising non-equilibrium systems, efficient energy transducers in the second step tend to keep the increase in entropy to a minimum by coupling the disequilibrium to other systems containing information. A well-known example is a grandfather clock which needs to be wound up only once a week: The mechanical energy contained in the wound spring is not released all at once, but in very small steps, each producing work turning the hands of the clock.

Even more dramatic are the metabolic systems of living cells. Coupled reactions ensure that high energy electrons moving across a whole series of organic molecules perform a maximum amount of chemical work before being returned, in numerous small steps, to the low energy state associated with oxygen – the earth's most important electron acceptor. These systems contain within them the slowly accumulated information of billions of years of an evolutionary process which tended to favour that which was more efficient, and to discard that which was less so. Thus, although the energy absorbed from the sun ultimately ends up as degraded heat, in the process the cell creates another cell – converting energy into information. That is, solar energy was used to transform relatively lowly organised, inert matter into a highly organised living system.

For a physical system such as a steam engine, the energy contained in a heated gas is not converted into work until it is contained and modulated by an engine which has accumulated within it a history of invention and information. By means of such an information-rich engine, it becomes possible to create a highly improbable event: The steam engine can segregate molecules so that a pocket of highly energetic molecules (in the form of steam) is placed next to a pocket of lower energy molecules, separated by a piston. It is this *sorting of molecules* into two pockets which constitutes the information input I. This is expended in the production of work and it is this which shows up as an increase in entropy.

In other words, the loss of information ΔI is reflected in the increase of entropy ΔS. The decrease in I represents a loss of information from the "informed" energy input. It does not represent a loss of the structural information contained within the energy transducer itself, which acts merely as a *catalyst*. In a steam engine, whereas the temperature T, pressure P, or volume of a gas V of the system as a whole may change, the structural, or inherent information of the system does not (except for a limited amount of wear and tear): A photovoltaic cell does not wear out by converting light energy into electrical energy. Nor does an ideal chemical catalyst. Even a steam engine which does wear out after many years, for practical purposes shows zero change in organisation during a single cycle in which there may be large changes in T, P or V.

Work in Biological Systems

Physicists have long recognised that functioning living systems produce work. All living systems are extremely complex when compared to the inert matter comprising the rest of the universe. "Complex" means that the system is highly organised, is polyphasic and contains vast stores of information. Even so "simple" a system as a plasmid – a mere naked string of nucleic acid – is a highly organised structure, representing, as it were, a form of "concentrated" biological information.

Advanced information systems such as living cells, provide the information needed to transform an input of energy into useful work under circumstances not possible in physical systems, which lack comparable levels of organisation. For example, the photosynthetic apparatus of a plant cell is part of a system able to dissociate water and strip electrons off hydrogen atoms at 25°C. In contrast, in an unorganised system, water needs to be heated to over 1,000°C before water molecules are destroyed by the violent collisions to create a plasma of ions and electrons. There is therefore an information input in plant photolysis which allows a temperature differential of about 1,000°C.

Photosynthetic systems are able to achieve this feat as a result of the ingenious arrangement of molecules (chlorophyll) able to absorb light, whose excited electrons move across a series of electron acceptors (pheophytin, quinones, etc) embedded in a membrane such that the electron ends up on the outer surface of the membrane, while the positive charge remains inside (see review by Youvan and Marrs 1987). The work performed which results in the accumulation of charges on opposite sides of a membrane, creates the potential energy for all further metabolic reactions on which the organisation and reproduction of living matter depend. It also represents the first of many steps which increase the information content of biological systems.

Similarly, the entire cellular machinery based on membranes and enzyme molecules permits a lowering of the activation energies required for the multitude of metabolic reactions (including the separation of H^+ and OH^- ions). The information (ie, organisation) contained within such molecules determines their ability to perform useful work, ie, work which organises the universe further.

We intuit that living things are very different from inorganic matter. What we perceive, even if only subconsciously, are the differences in structure and function. The *structure* of life when compared to inorganic matter, is much more complex – it is much richer in organisation. The *function* of living matter appears to relate to its ability to increase the organisation of this universe: A cell ingests dead matter to create another cell. An oak tree sows its acorns and converts soil into a forest. A cow eats grass and produces a calf. This is truly miraculous. The second law of thermodynamics may be omnipresent; however, whenever entropy is increased as a *by-product* of metabolic reactions, it is more than compensated for by applying much of the "free energy" obtained from these metabolic reactions, to achieving a general reduction in entropy. Thus we see the evolution from a barren planet earth three billion years ago, to a fertile globe where almost the entire surface is covered with living things.

Living systems are energy transducers which use information

1. **to perform work more efficiently,**
2. **to convert one form of energy into another, and**
3. **to convert energy into information.**

Reassessing the Work Equations

The structural information content of energy transducers, though a vital component of any physical change producing useful work, is the same at the end of a process as it was at the beginning. This is probably the reason why it has been overlooked or ignored in the past.

If the importance of the structural information of energy transducers is easy to overlook, the same cannot be said for the kinetic information. Information machines, when acting as energy transducers may convert a certain amount of energy into kinetic information. This is particularly true for steam engines: The amount of kinetic information produced from the heat input is too large to ignore.

As already discussed earlier, traditional physics has invented two accounting devices to cover this situation: potential energy, and entropy. The kinetic information created by the steam engine when it has produced an asymmetric distribution of high and low energy water molecules in the two chambers separated by a piston is called *potential energy*. The apparent loss of a part of this energy, which really represents a loss of kinetic information, ie, that part of the information which has been degraded to heat, is called *entropy*.

The reason for reiterating this matter is to emphasise the point that it becomes necessary to redefine the "work equations" in terms of, not only an input of energy, but also an input of information. That is, somehow we must rework the work equations to take account of the fact that devices which produce useful work, whether a photosynthesising cell or a steam locomotive, do so not only because of an input of energy, but also because of an input of information.

Efficient energy transducers, whether a steam engine or a photosynthesising cell, are structurally organised in such a way so as to maximise the output of useful work W for any given energy input Q. The structural organisation I_s, in some, as yet unknown manner, provides the *information input* I_i which modulates the energy input. Visualise the difference of information inputs between heated steam in the cylinder of a functioning steam engine and the same in an open pot of boiling water.

Work which results in a reduction of entropy – "useful" work W_u – must be some function of this information input I_i. Obviously all work output is a function of the energy input Q. Therefore,

$$W_u = f[Q, I_i] \tag{7.1}$$

This relationship must be viewed in the context of our earlier discussion about the information content of energy itself: Q may make a substantial information contribution in its own right. For example, electromagnetic radiation is a highly organised form of energy, being produced by highly organised, resonant structures and fields. At the other extreme is heat with no information content, requiring a large information input from something as sophisticated as a steam engine in order to produce useful work. Thermodynamics began with a study of steam engines.

The structural information contained by a steam engine – that is, its I_s – performs at least two information functions: (1) It sets the stage for creating what is generally called potential energy, but which we equate to kinetic information I_k, and (2) it provides a countervailing force to minimise the loss of I_k to entropy.

In a steam engine the first of these is the *kinetic information*, measurable as the potential energy at its peak, when the differential between the compressed steam on one side of the piston, and the partial vacuum of the condensed water vapour on the other side, represents the maximum disequilibrium. The greater this quantity, the greater the kinetic information, hence the greater must have been the information input I_i.

The second, the countervailing force, is provided in a steam engine by the walls of the cylinder and the piston, which restrict the movement of the molecules. The walls force the molecules back into the chamber rather than letting them escape as they would if they were in a pot of boiling water. The movement of the piston alters the path length of molecules travelling parallel to the direction in which the piston is moving, bringing about a "unidirectional cooling". This constitutes part of the process of superimposing information on energy. Coupling the piston to drive wheels also represents a part of the countervailing force. However, the movement of the drive wheel represents the energy output. Because the output is in the form of mechanical energy, it constitutes "informed" (ie, organised) energy which may be utilised for engaging in further "useful" work (eg, generating electricity or transporting goods).

In the steam engine, the above processes – creating a disequilibrium situation and providing a countervailing force – constitute the basic principles upon which all energy transducers operate. The combination of these two reflects the information inputs of such devices. However, a steam engine represents the extreme in energy transducers because the input is heat – a low grade form of energy which, unlike all other forms of energy, contains no information at all. It starts, therefore, with an input of low-grade energy and transduces it into mechanical energy capable of performing useful work. It does this by organising things – by adding information – derived from the structural information properties of its design.

It becomes virtually impossible to measure all the inputs of information that go into designing and constructing a steam engine. It represents the summation of the history of technology, not only in terms of the history of steam engines, but also metallurgy, machine tooling, factory design, etc, plus the information contained by the raw materials, the energy supplied (mechanical, electrical, etc), and in particular, the skills and education of the workers, engineers and managers who produce the steel, the various components, and finally the finished engine. At present, to attempt to quantify the summation of all these various information inputs appears a hopeless task.

We therefore attempt an alternative approach: To assess the value of the total information inputs I_i by ascertaining their effect on the output – specifically by looking at the efficiency η of converting the energy input Q into useful work W_u:*

Efficiency is measured by the ratio of work output to heat input:

$$\eta = W/Q \tag{7.2}$$

which can be measured by comparing the caloric value of the heat input, with the work obtained. The greater this fraction, ie, the more of the heat that has been converted to work, the greater the efficiency.

The maximum possible efficiency can be calculated from the relationship between the temperature input T_{in} and the temperature of the system's surroundings T_{out}. In the case of a steam engine this is the ratio of the temperature of the boiler and the temperature of the engine's environment.

$$\eta_{max} = 1 - T_{out}/T_{in} \tag{7.3}$$

We now assume that efficiency is a function of the information input I_i provided by the structural information of the steam engine. Specifically, we compare the *actual* efficiency with the *maximum* possible efficiency:

$$\eta_{act} / \eta_{max} = f(I_i) \tag{7.4}$$

and suggest that the relationship could possibly be such that as the information input approaches infinity, the actual efficiency approaches the maximum possible, while when the input is zero, so is the actual efficiency. Such a relationship could be expressed by:

---

* The author is indebted to Drs N. McEwan and J. Noras for discussions leading to the appropriate calculations.

$$\eta_{act} / \eta_{max} = 1 - e^{-cI_i} \tag{7.5}$$

or

$$I_i = -\frac{1}{c} \log [1 - \eta_{act} / \eta_{max}] \tag{7.6}$$

However, these two equations are not the only ones possible for describing the relationship between information inputs and efficiency. The problem remains an open question for information thermodynamicists to solve.

Another possible approach to ascertaining the relative value of the information inputs is by comparing the entropy outcomes. That is, by measuring the ratio of the difference in entropy between the system performing useful work per given unit of energy, and the same amount of energy being completely dissipated. Using the conversion factor derived at the end of chapter 4 (1 J/K = 10^{23} bits), it would become possible – by measuring the ratio of the differences in entropy outcomes – to ascribe a value to the information inputs.

Measuring the Information Content of Electrical Work

As indicated above, the steam engine represents the extreme case for energy transducers because the input of energy into the system is heat, a form of energy devoid of information. Information thermodynamicists might do better, therefore, to focus on a system such as an electric motor in which the energy input consists of electrical energy, a highly organised form of energy, ie, energy with a significant information input to start with.

In an electric motor the efficiency is easily ascertained not only by comparing the electrical energy input with the mechanical energy output, but also by measuring the amount of energy lost to (degraded to) heat. The less lost to heat, the greater the efficiency of the system, and the greater must have been the information input into the system. This information input I_i is a function of two aspects of the structural information I_s contained by the motor: The first is its architecture – the shape of the magnet and its poles, how the armature is wound, etc, the second is determined by the nature of the materials used, both in the magnetic core, and in the conductors – a matter which is currently of great interest as high temperature superconductors come on stream.

An electric current traversing a conductor leads to another important consideration based on the argument stated in chapter 4: If one joule per degree is equivalent to approximately 10^{23} bits, since one electron volt equals 1.6×10^{-19} joules, one may calculate that one electron volt per degree, is equivalent to 1.6×10^4 bits:

$$1 \text{ ev/K} = 1.6 \times 10^4 \text{ bits} \tag{7.7}$$

A flow of electrons, ie, an electric current, is measured in amperes. If the above considerations prove to be valid, then per K an electric current of one ampere flowing in an electric circuit would involve the transfer of information at a rate of approximately 10^{23} bits/volt/second. This would be consistent with the idea that a movement of charges brings about a change in the organisation of the universe, and is dependent on temperature. On the other hand, if all the electrical work ends up as heat dissipated across a resistor, then, as discussed above, one could measure this as information lost to entropy.

Unfortunately, even in a system such as an electric motor – a system much more amenable to studying the relationships between structural information I_s and the actual information inputs I_i – it will be some time before it will be possible to define, in any quantitative way, the I_s/I_i relationship.

On the other hand, by looking at diverse systems it might become possible to ascertain whether the constant c in equations (7.5) and (7.6) has universal applicability or whether it is unique for each particular energy transducing system.

Finally, there is another aspect of electrical work which is worth noting: The precise relationship between the *input of work W*, and *the creation of kinetic information I_k*:

The potential energy U of an electrical system such as a charged battery, is equal to the amount of work required to produce the potential energy. That is:

$$W = U \tag{7.8}$$

In a highly organised system such as a battery, the *charged state* represents a thermodynamically highly improbable condition, low in entropy, obviously at some distance from equilibrium. The information content, therefore, is high. This would be consistent with the assumption that potential energy is a form of information, to be precise, kinetic information I_k. Equation (7.8), $W = U$, indicates that as far as electrical work is concerned, the kinetic information I_k produced is exactly equal to the amount of work applied. Such a charged battery, therefore, represents evidence that *the kinetic information content of a system is directly proportional to the amount of work required to produce it.*

Literature Cited

DC Youvan and BL Marrs (1987) Molecular mechanisms of photosynthesis, *Sci. Am.* 256(6):42–48.

· 8 ·

Summary and Concluding Remarks

Introduction

This book comprises the first step toward the development of a general theory of information. Its main thesis is that "information" is not merely a product of the human mind – a mental construct to help us understand the world we inhabit – rather, information is a property of the universe, as real as are matter and energy.

The second theme derives directly from the first: If "information" has as much physical reality as do matter and energy, then the perceptions and constructs of the physical sciences need to be re-examined. The rest of the book, therefore, represents an exploration of "information physics".

The Basic Propositions

The basic propositions of information physics may be summarised as follows:

1. The structure of the universe consists of at least three components: matter, energy, *and* information; information is as intrinsic a part of the universe as are matter and energy.
2. Physical information is related to at least three factors: First, and foremost, it is reflected by organisation. Second, it is a function of thermodynamic improbability. Third, the information content of a system is a function of the amount of "useful" work required to create it.
   - 2A. Any system which possesses organisation, either in temporal or in spatial terms, manifest or inherent,

contains information. What mass is to the manifestation of matter, and heat is to energy, organisation is to information.

2B. Information I is the reciprocal of Boltzmann's probability function W, and thereby is related exponentially to the negative of entropy S. Changes in entropy measure both changes in thermodynamic probability and changes in organisation. The relation between entropy and information is provided by the general equation:

$$S = k \ln(I_0/I)$$

2C. Other things being equal, the information content of a system is determined by the amount of "useful" work required to produce it. Information processing is a form of work. Per degree (K), one joule of energy, if it were possible to convert it into pure information, would be equivalent to approximately 10^{23} bits.

3. Physical information may exist in many forms: Time, distance, and direction, the constants of equations describing the physical world, the information properties of particles of matter, the information properties of various forms of energy – all represent various forms of information. Important to the analysis of physical systems performing work is the distinction between *structural information* which reflects the organisation of matter and energy, and *kinetic information* which represents the information acquired by a system as it enters into a thermodynamically less probable, disequilibrium situation.

4. Energy and information are interconvertible. In a disequilibrium situation, potential energy is equivalent to kinetic information. In charging up a battery,

$$1 \text{ ev/K} = 1.6 \times 10^4 \text{ bits}$$

5. The increase in entropy associated with energetic processes reflects the degradation of the applied (kinetic) information into heat. One entropy unit equals approximately 10^{23} bits/mole, or

$$1 \text{ J/K} = 10^{23} \text{ bits}$$

6. Heat is a form of energy lacking information. The term "heat" as used in the present context is equivalent to the concept of uncorrelated phonons in a crystal, or the random

motion of molecules in a gas. It represents vibrational energy which tends to *disorganise* systems.

7. The application of heat to a system requires a further input of information (applied information) in order to obtain useful work out of the system. The output of work in any process is a function of the product of mass or energy, and information.
8. All forms of energy other than heat, contain an information component.
9. Physical constants reflect nature's algorithms. They reflect an ordering of physical systems or events. The human perception of that natural order is reflected in how such constants are expressed mathematically.

Historical Perspective

The concept of "energy" as something distinct, with a physical reality of its own, is a relatively recent phenomenon in human history. The systematic exploration of "forces" began only after such forces were apparently "created" by human invention: Galileo was a military engineer studying the trajectories of cannon balls; similarly, Carnot and his nineteenth-century colleagues founded thermodynamics only after a century of experience with steam engines.

Experimentation fosters the manipulation of physical parameters. It is a way of gaining new experiences. Faraday was such an experimenter. He described and interpreted his experiments on electricity and magnetism in precise, if not mathematical terms. However, just as Newton elaborated brilliantly on the forces described by Galileo, so did Maxwell subsequently elaborate on Faraday's experiences.*

We are in a comparable historical situation today. The concept of "information" as something distinct, with an independent reality of its own, reflects our more recent historical experiences. Three are of particular relevance:

First, there were the experiences of the telegraph, telephone, and radio engineers charged with the job of maximising transmission efficiency. It is no coincidence that among the first

---

* It has been said that Faraday, when asked what was his greatest discovery, replied "Maxwell". (Maxwell had been working in his laboratory as a lowly assistant.)

to treat "information" as an independent, abstract quantity were engineers such as R.V.L. Hartley, who in 1928 defined information as a quantity and provided an equation for its measurement (as reviewed by Cherry 1978).

Second, most important, we have now had over four decades of experience with electronic computers. These devices, initially designed as aids for solving lengthy and tedious mathematical problems, ie, as computational aids, rapidly evolved into information processing systems of increasing complexity and sophistication. They made plain that human information could not only be stored, but manipulated outside the human brain. This was a dramatic difference.

As long as human information was something static, as in books in a library, it did not seem to arouse much wonder and excitement. Psychologically, information appeared as something dead. The experience of librarians, or of the enlightened eighteenth-century encyclopaedists – the experience of trying to classify human information – never led to the suggestion that information might exist as an independent force in the universe.

The computer has changed our perception of information as something purely static. Inside a computer, information appears to have a dynamic of its own – it appears to have life. The excitement of this new experience quickly entered our common culture: Words and phrases such as "input" and "output", "information processing", "down time", etc, became applied to non-computer situations. Psychologists began to consider the human brain as a highly complex, biological information processor.

The third significant strand in our recent historical experience derives from the findings of the molecular biologists. The unequivocal demonstration that complex molecules such as DNA comprise the carrier of genetic information, crowns our collective experience. This experience actually spans millenia of practical animal and plant breeding, as well as the common observation that children tend to resemble their parents.

This genetic information, transmitted from generation to generation, turns out to reside in an inanimate, aperiodic crystal. Both the crystal storing this information, and the code, preceded the appearance of the human brain by at least a thousand million years. Obviously information may exist in forms wholly separate and distinct from human beings.

Why Has Information Been Overlooked?

If information is a basic property of the universe, why has it, prior to now, escaped the notice of the physicists?

There are at least two reasons: First, as already discussed, until the emergence of knowledge engineering as a discipline there was no pressing need for defining and studying information in its own right. The nearest thing to a need for handling information as an abstract entity in its own right, occurred earlier in the twentieth century when the telecommunications engineers were confronted with the problem of transporting it.

The second reason why it has been so easy to overlook the information component is that it is ever-present and obvious. Its very ubiquitousness and obviousness allows one to treat it as "a given". Distance and time are ever-present and obvious. They are the "given" which allow us to describe motion. And the description of motion is the cardinal principle on which the science of physics was founded, and which still permeates that discipline today.

Related to the above is the fact that information and energy are so readily interconvertible. Thus the physicist could almost always fall back on restating the mathematical description of various phenomena and processes involving changes in information in terms of changes in energy. Only occasionally did the energy seem to disappear and require the invention of new terms like entropy, or potential energy, to keep the ledger balanced.

The main reason, however, was the first: There was no pressing need to look for information – not until the advent of advanced information processing systems required a general theory of information.

The Need for Models and Theories

All higher forms of intelligence have in their memory store, some map – some model – of the universe. The evolution, both biologically and in humans, culturally, of a view of the universe – a cosmology – has been thoughtfully explored by Geza Szamosi (1986). The need to create a mental map, accounts for the fact that all human cultures exhibit considerable inventiveness in creating a mental construct of the universe. A great deal of theory goes into these constructs to explain a whole host of phenomena, ranging from illness to the weather. Usually such theories rely on the existence of supernatural beings, endowed with supernatural powers, carrying on a variety of otherwise human activities. In contrast, modern science has been able to devise a cosmology which eschews anthropomorphic models and whose predictive value, ranging from illness to weather, has proved much more accurate. The understanding of infectious illnesses, allowing effective prevention and treatment, is probably one of the greatest victories of modern science and probably accounts for much of its success in being embraced by other cultures in almost all parts of the world.

There is another aspect however, to model building. That is, the use of mathematics as a model builder. As it developed, mathematics began to provide more and better models. Even more startling, it provided models for phenomena not yet discovered. For example, Dirac's mathematical equations implied negative energy states and anticipated the existence of anti-matter. Thus modern science was able not only to devise theories which could explain existing phenomena, but theories which could explain phenomena not yet discovered. Traditional model building may be said to involve the observation of unexplained phenomena in search of a theory. In contrast, the power of model building in modern science also contains a method which creates unexplained theories in search of phenomena. Thus history is filled with examples of philosophers and scientists developing abstract theories which at the time, although elegant in their own right, seemed to have no practical application but which subsequently became crucial for developing some other, practical field of application. Boolean algebra and its subsequent utility to computing, represents one such example.

The Relevance of Information Physics for a General Theory of Information

Information physics will become an established and fruitful science when the material presented in this book has been properly quantified on the one hand, and experimentally or observationally verified on the other. At this point in history, information physics needs a Clerk Maxwell.

There is, however, another consideration: The need to develop a general theory of information. To create such a theory, we need to start with the most fundamental aspect of information. And the most fundamental aspect of information is that it is not a construct of the human mind but a basic property of the universe. Any general theory of information must begin by studying the physical properties of information as they manifest themselves in the universe. This must be done before attempting to understand the various, and much more complex forms of human information. The next step must involve an examination of the evolution of information systems beyond physical systems – first in the biological, then in the human, cultural sphere.

As information physics develops, hopefully, there will emerge new insights which will advance our understanding of information. However, there are already certain basic principles which have become apparent. Perhaps the most important of these is the role of bonds or links in determining organisation. This emerges from an examination of the phenomena associated with changes in entropy (see chapters 3–5): Increases in entropy are invariably associated with a loss of organisation. The most dramatic changes such as the melting of a crystal, or the vaporisation of a liquid, occur when one particular class of bonding breaks down completely and the body of matter is fragmented into smaller, uncoordinated units. If one considers the range of discontinuities from a crystal of ice to a quagma this breakdown in organisation becomes apparent: Crystals of ice, liquid water, steam, atoms and ions of hydrogen and oxygen, electrons and ions only, nucleons and atomic fragments, nucleons, quarks. At each point, the loss of organisation involves a disappearance of bonds linking the subunits into more complex, more organised structures. It is the disappearance of these bonds which represent the loss of information associated with the marked increases in entropy at these discontinuities.

Therefore, if one were to attempt to assess the absolute value of the information content of a crystal of ice, one needs to know the information value of the bonds linking the molecules of water into a stable, crystalline structure, the bonds linking the atoms of hydrogen and oxygen to create a molecule of water, the bonds linking the orbital electrons to their atomic nuclei, the bonds linking the various nucleons into atoms of oxygen, and finally, the bonds linking the quarks into the nucleons comprising the atoms of hydrogen and oxygen. In addition, one needs to know the information value of the various types of quarks, and finally, one needs to know the total number of each of the different forms of quarks contained by the crystal of ice. That is, if quarks do represent the basic units of information (which they probably do not), their total number constitutes one of the factors determining the total information content of the crystal.

Whereas it is obvious that the information content of a system is a function of the *number* of information sub-units comprising the system, the information physics of entropy (in contrast to the thermodynamics of entropy) indicates clearly that it is the *linking* of simpler units into more complex systems which is the basis of organisation.

In the light of the above considerations, if the first axiom of a general theory of information is:

Information is a basic property of the universe,

the second axiom must be:

The information contained by a system is a function of the linkages binding simpler, into more complex units.

A derivative conclusion of this second axiom is:

The universe is organised into a hierarchy of information levels.

That is, the internal structure of the universe not only consists of information, but the information is itself organised into layers of increasing complexity. In a subsequent work (*Beyond Chaos*) we will explore this complexity and introduce the biological concept of "differentiation" into the analysis. Suffice it here merely to point to fig. 3.2, plotting information against entropy, and the discussions in chapter 4 relating to this graph, to remind ourselves that there appears to be no upper limit to the amount of information possible. This reflects the fact that information may not only organise matter and energy, information may organise *information* – a process which occurs, for example, in our brains – and in our computers.

A further important information concept is that of *resonance*. The characteristics of transmitted physical information, eg, electromagnetic radiation, or sound, are determined by the structural information of the transmitter in the form of its resonance. To absorb and process such transmitted information effectively, it becomes necessary to attune the receiver to be able to provide the appropriate resonance for reception. A comparable state of affairs applies when trying to communicate human information.

Thus, the above principles, although applied in the present work to physical information systems such as atoms and crystals, will also prove to be applicable to biological and social systems – even to human information systems such as computers and language.

Some Concluding Thoughts

The material discussed in this book represents merely an *introduction* to an alternative view of physical phenomena. It involves a reinterpretation of well- established analyses. Some of it makes intuitive sense; some of it may prove to be wrong. Nevertheless, it is a beginning.

There was a time when light was measured in foot candles, heat in calories, sound in decibels, electricity in volts, etc. The study of information is, similarly, still in its infancy: The multitudinous forms of information will, initially, continue to be described in different kinds of units such as bits, metres, seconds, electric charges, nucleotides, letters, etc.

Another shortcoming of the present work is its lack of predictive power. Einstein's theory of relativity predicted that the gravitational field of the sun would bend light rays, therefore one should be able to see stars behind the sun. Observations during the next solar eclipse confirmed this. Were it possible to devise an experiment which would make an approaching black star "visible" along the lines discussed in the appendix, then the *infon theory* would receive strong support.

Popper's dictum on being able to falsify a theory is well known. Therefore one could argue that most of the material presented here is not scientific. However, if much of it is unproven, much of it makes sense. That some of it is speculative, cannot be disputed; yet it brings together diverse observations, creating a coherent pattern. It also addresses itself to some current paradoxes. Again, one may point to a historical analogy – the theory of evolution proposed by Darwin and Wallace. At the time, the science of genetics did not exist and no experimental verification was possible. Yet the theory of evolution reinterpreted, and made sense out of, a large body of data without being falsifiable at the time.

The introduction of information as a basic factor in the analysis of physical phenomena, creates a vast number of opportunities for reinterpreting existing observations and theories. A number of currently held beliefs will need to be modified and in some cases, discarded: Information has physical reality; information is interconvertible with energy; potential energy is a form of information; entropy is inversely related to information and, as a statement of the information content of the system, may become a negative quantity (thereby apparently violating the Third Law of Thermodynamics); the coulomb represents a unit of information, while the ampere represents units of information on the move – changing the organisation of the universe.

Actually, the speculations presented in the appendix go much deeper and, if correct, will require further paradigm shifts. For example, the implications of a theory of information for particle physics, suggest that the basic structure of the universe consists not only of fermions and bosons, but of *infons* as well. That is, there exists a class of particles which possesses neither mass nor momentum, but whose movement is intimately concerned with reorganising the internal structure of matter. *Infons* would include particles such as phonons, excitons, and the holes left in atomic shells by ejected electrons. Therefore not only may matter and energy exist in particulate form – so may information.

Once information physics is established, it will have an immediate impact on thermodynamics. All three laws need to be reinterpreted and broadened along the lines discussed in the previous pages. The introduction of information as a parameter will allow a much clearer insight into the nature and limitations of thermodynamic processes. Conversely, it is because thermodynamics has always, if unwittingly, concerned itself with the relationship between energy changes and information changes, that thermodynamics has provided information physics with a handle on how to quantify the conversion of energy into information.

Since it was Boltzmann who clarified the concept that entropy represents an expression of the probability of a system's state – and, by implication, its state of order or disorder – it would be fitting to end the explorations presented above with a quote from his *Lectures on Gas Theory* (part II, 1898, p. 447, translated by Brush 1964). In discussing the cosmic implications of the second law of thermodynamics, Boltzmann considers "the heat death of each single world", ie, the "unidirectional change of the entire universe from a definite initial state to a fixed state". He then comments: "Obviously no one would consider such speculations as important discoveries or even – as did the ancient philosophers – as the highest purpose of science. However it is doubtful that one should despise them as completely idle. Who knows whether they may not broaden the horizon of our circle of ideas, and by stimulating thought, advance the understanding of the facts of experience?"

It is in the spirit of advancing our understanding of the facts of experience that the preceding pages (and the appendixes) are offered, with the hope that these discussions will indeed broaden the horizon of the circle of ideas first defined by Boltzmann, then extended by Schrödinger.

Literature Cited

SG Brush (1964) *Ludwig Boltzmann: Lectures on Gas Theory*, University of California Press, Berkeley.

C Cherry (1978) *On Human Communication*, 3rd edn, The MIT Press, Cambridge, Mass.

G Szamosi (1986) *The Twin Dimensions: Inventing Time and Space*, McGraw-Hill, New York.

Appendixes

In the preceding part of the book we have explored the basic propositions of information physics. Although many of the ideas expressed may appear novel, and although many questions have been left unanswered, on the whole, the ideas and information presented are cogent and internally consistent. Details may have to be adjusted and restated, measurements and calculation will need to be carried out, but on the whole – in the author's opinion – the cardinal features of information physics will stand the test of time.

There are other matters, however: Establishing information physics as a legitimate scientific discipline has a host of implications for the entire field of physics. Many of these are quite startling. The author would like to explore some of these, not because such speculations will necessarily prove true, but because they are interesting.

It should be emphasised that the speculations presented in this appendix are wholly independent of the validity of the basic propositions discussed earlier. Should all the speculations in the succeeding pages prove false, that would not alter the soundness of the basic tenets of information physics as discussed in the preceding. On the other hand, the thoughts expressed in the appendixes derive logically from the basic propositions posited earlier, and therefore are worthy of further exploration. As such, they create an alternative view of the universe, both macroscopic and microscopic.

· *Appendix A* ·

Speculations on Electromagnetic Radiation and Particles of Information

---

Information Electronics

The idea that gravitational potential energy and electrical potential energy are equivalent, flows naturally from the fact that the law of attraction between charges is very similar to the law of gravitation (although there is an enormous difference in the strength of the two forces). If a spring, hung from a ceiling, is attached to a weight and the weight is pulled down and then released, an oscillation is generated as the weight bobs up and down. Such an oscillating system alternates between kinetic and potential energy.

Given the equivalency of potential energy and kinetic information, such a system may also be viewed as oscillating between a high (kinetic) *information* and a high (kinetic) *energy* state.

An electrical circuit with an inductance and capacitance in series parallels exactly the mechanical system described above. In the electrical circuit the voltage across the capacitor is at maximum when the current is zero, and drops to zero as the current becomes maximum. It is obvious that as the voltage rises to a maximum, then drops to zero, so does the potential energy.

On this basis it becomes possible to reinterpret an oscillating electrical circuit in terms of a system alternating between two states: A high kinetic energy, and a high kinetic *information* state. The first is characterised by the dynamic flow of current; the latter by a static state in which no current flows.

However, the dynamic – the high kinetic energy state when the current flow is at a maximum – is not a *zero information* state. Associated with the current flow is a substantial amount of information: First, the current flows in a specific direction. Second, since the current consists of moving charges, and since each charge comprises a unit of information, the current itself involves the movement of information. Third, the moving electric field, a highly organised form of energy, generates a magnetic field, another highly organised force. Thus an oscillating electric circuit exhibits not only oscillations in the intensity and direction of the current, but also in terms of the level and nature of its kinetic information.

Finally, the frequency of oscillation is a function of resonance. Resonance is entirely dependent on the structural information properties of the electrical circuit – the size of the capacitor plates, the nature of the dielectric material, the number of turns in the induction coil, etc. The dimension of this structural information determines the mathematical values of the kinetic information.

The idea that a resonating electric circuit fluctuates between various energy and information states can provide an alternative analysis of electromagnetic systems, in particular, electromagnetic radiation.

Magnetism

Magnetism is obviously a highly organised force: Atoms or molecules arrange themselves so that their dipoles become aligned. Iron filings, sprinkled randomly on a surface become organised into patterns. A magnetic field, therefore, exemplifies a piece of "organised space": Under its influence it causes matter to become organised or reorganised. That is, a magnetic field is capable of imparting information.

If an electric current may be viewed as an energetic flow of information, then a magnetic force, directly transduced from such a flow of informed energy, also possesses a high level of information.

The structural information contained by an electric motor makes possible the conversion of an electrical force to a magnetic, and then to a mechanical force which, in turn may produce useful work. The interconversion of one form of energy into another is accompanied by the transfer of information. Unlike an electric current flowing across a resistor in which the information is degraded owing to the non-specific interaction between electrons and matter (creating non-specific heat), an electric current flowing through an induction coil transfers its information to the magnetic flux created. Electromagnetic phenomena therefore involve energy which contains a very high level of information.

Information and Electromagnetic Radiation

The energy of light is dependent on its wavelength. One measures wavelength in terms of distance. Conversely, one may assess the energy of light in terms of frequency, which one measures as pulses per unit time. But, as we discussed earlier, any arrangement within space and time implies some pattern of organisation, hence information. Therefore light must contain information.

Information must be a key element in organising the atom, its nucleus, its sub-nuclear components, and its electronic shell structure. When light is absorbed by an atom, there is a reorganisation in its electronic shell as an electron is moved out into a higher energy level. Such a reorganisation implies that not only has the atom undergone a change in its energy state, but also a change in its information state.

If the absorption of light leads to a change in the atom's information state, then either light contains information which may be transferred to the atom, or the energy of light may be converted into information, or both mechanisms operate.

If a photon contains information, then perhaps a photon is not a fundamental particle after all. Rather, it may be made up of two components: first, an energy component and second an information component. The two alternately being transformed from one into the other as part of an oscillating system.

The frequency of an oscillating system such as a musical instrument producing sound, or an electronic system producing pulses of electricity, is determined by the resonance of the system. The resonance, as discussed earlier, is a function of the organisation of the system – in other words, of its structural information content. Thus the *frequency* of oscillation reflects an input of information rather than an input of energy.

The above reiterates the concept that the properties of an oscillating electric circuit, consisting of a capacitor and an induction coil, involve not only oscillations on the part of the electromagnetic energy produced by the system, but also of its information. Thus an electromagnetic wave emitted, for example, by a radio transmitter, consists of not one, but of *two* sets of oscillations: The first one is well known – the oscillating electric field alternating with an oscillating magnetic field. The axes of these two fields are at right angles to each other, and both are at right angles to the direction of propagation. The maxima of field strength of the two oscillating forces, electric and magnetic, are 90° out of phase.

To this first, rather complicated but integrated oscillation, we need to add another: The regular alternation of information and energy. Maximum information correlates with maximum potential energy and therefore correlates with the electric field. Maximum energy correlates with maximum current flow, ie, maximum kinetic energy, and therefore correlates with the magnetic field. If this is true, the energon and infon may continuously interconvert during the propagation of a photon.

Light as "Escaped Resonance" Quanta?

Atomic structures contain comparable resonance structures involving capacitance (the separation of protons and electrons), and inductance (the spin of the nucleus and the orbiting electrons). A photon emitted by an atom could be viewed as a piece of "escaped resonance". That is, a light quantum is a piece of atomic energy/ information engaged in a stable oscillation which allows it to propagate across space. Although it has no mass, it has a direction and its velocity is intrinsic to its electro-magnetic information state as described by Maxwell's equations. Both the initial direction of the photon, and its original frequency is determined by the resonating energy/ information state of the emitting atom.

It may be difficult to envisage an oscillating blob consisting of energy and information, neither of which has mass, moving through space. One of the best ways to give a feeling for such an entity is to refer to the computer game called "Life" devised in 1970 by John Horton Conway at Cambridge. The game, a sort of video kaleidoscope, is a world unto itself – William

Poundstone (1985) has described it as "a window onto an alternate universe."

The rules of "Life" determine the (unpredictable) events on the screen so that the game plays itself: The situation at one moment determines the situation at the next. Each cell on a video screen may be in one of two states: on or off. Each square has eight other cells surrounding it. Whether an "on" cell remains on, or is turned off at the next round, is determined by the on/off states of its various neighbours and by the rules imposed on the system by the player. If for example the rule is that a square turns on if its neighbour to the left is on, but turns off if its neighbour to the right is on, then the tendency of the lighted pattern will be to move to the right.

One particularly fascinating pattern has been called the "Glider", a five-cell unit which creeps across the screen like an amoeba, changing its shape as it goes. It assumes four different phases: Two phases are the shifted mirror images of the other two; any phase is reproduced exactly four generations later, at which time it will have moved one cell diagonally. In other words, here is an example of an oscillating system which possesses no mass, and moves. Unlike a photon, however, it is not self sufficient. The Glider requires a continuous input of energy (the electrons falling on the screen of the cathode ray tube), and information (the rules stored in the computer's memory and applied by it).

Furthermore, the Glider moves across a well-defined medium – the fluorescent screen of the cathode ray tube. We do not know of any comparable medium which transmits light.

If one views a photon as a piece of "escaped resonance", then it becomes natural that a properly tuned resonance system should be able to capture a photon intact. Radio receiving circuits are designed to trap radio waves. Pigment molecules trap light. The higher the energy/information content of the photon, the greater the impact on the receiver. In a radio receiver the energy/information is initially converted into flows of electrons. In an atom, the energy/information added by a photon results in the reorganisation of the electronic shell structure. In all instances some of the energy/information is degraded to heat and the entropy increased. However, in all instances that involve the resonance absorptions of a photon, the absorbing body gains in both energy *and* information.

May Information Be Particulate?

One of the features which made Times Square in New York a centre of attraction was the electric sign alongside the Times Building. The latest news bulletins flashed along the sign, moving like a gigantic ticker tape – bringing, over the years, entertainment and enlightenment to millions of passers-by.

As the letters and words migrated along the sign, the illusion was created that the light bulbs were moving across the screen as discrete entities. The light bulbs, of course, did not move at all. They were completely stationary. However, because they represented binary information devices, their on/off states allowed *patterns* of light to traverse the length of the sign.

Such patterns of light, moving across a fixed distance at a fixed rate exhibit both frequency and wavelength – easily discernible if, instead of words, just a series of bars, or uppercase letter "I"s, were moving across the sign. Such waves do *not* represent waves of *energy*: The energy is confined to the flow of electricity in the light bulb circuits. They do, however, represent waves of *information*.

Our universe is filled with examples in which changes in organisation patterns – by definition, changes in information states – result in the appearance of waves or particles. Phase waves, for example, represent information superimposed on a carrier wave. Such waves, superimposed on light waves could, in theory, move faster (or slower) than the electromagnetic waves which carry them. Inside a crystal, "holes" may appear and move as if they were particles. As with the Times Square sign, the holes do not actually move. It is the sequential opening up and filling of holes which produces the illusion that the holes are moving. Thus, massless particles like phonons and excitons, thought to be important in explaining the behaviour of electrons in superconductivity states, represent particles of information. Like the light bulbs on the Times Square sign, *the behaviour of phonons and excitons represents a particle-like manifestation of gross changes in organisation*, as *patterns* of information flow across the system.

Infons

It is the purpose of the rest of this section to explore the possibility that like light, and associated with it, information may also appear to exist in particulate form: That is, that there exists a class of hypothetical particles which consist of only information. Such "infons" might not show up in traditional physical experiments since such particles would possess neither mass nor energy – they could, however, manifest their effect by changes in organisation.

Let us begin with an exploration of the interconvertibility of energy and information:

$$E = m_0c^2/ \sqrt{(1 - v^2/c^2)} \tag{A.1}$$

If a particle is massless, ie, $m_0 = 0$, then equation (A.1) implies that unless the particle is travelling at the speed of light c, its energy must be zero. That is, if $m_0 = 0$:

$$E = (0)c^2 / \sqrt{(1-v^2/c^2)} = 0 \tag{A.2}$$

However, if the particle is travelling at the speed of light (v=c), then $v^2/c^2 = 1$. If $v^2/c^2 = 1$, then E in equation (A.1) becomes indeterminate, ie:

$$E = (0)c^2/ \sqrt{(1-1)} = 0/0 \tag{A.3}$$

This means E can have a value, but it cannot be determined by means of equation (A.1).

A similar argument can be made for "relativistic momentum" p which is given by the following equation:

$$p = m_0v/ \sqrt{(1 - v^2/c^2)} \tag{A.4}$$

Now consider a massless particle moving at a velocity other than that of light c. It would possess neither energy nor momentum. Yet, in theory, such a particle could exist. Like a photon, it would possess no rest mass; unlike a photon, however, it would not travel with a velocity of c, and therefore possess no momentum either. Nevertheless, it could possess velocity; therefore it could represent a moving unit consisting of pure information.

Let us explore the properties of such a hypothetical particle further. The linear momentum of a photon, as given in equation (A.4), may also be expressed as:

$$p = h\nu/c \tag{A.5}$$

where h = Planck's constant
and ν = frequency of the photon

The relationship between frequency ν and the wavelength λ is given by the equation:

$$\nu = c/\lambda \qquad (A.6)$$

therefore, by substituting (A.6) in (A.5), we obtain

$$p = h/\lambda \qquad (A.7)$$

or

$$\lambda = h/p \qquad (A.8)$$

Substituting (A.4) in (A.8), we obtain:

$$\lambda = h \,/\, [m_0 v/\sqrt{(1 - v^2/c^2)}] \qquad (A.9)$$
$$= h\sqrt{(1 - v^2/c^2)} \,/\, m_0 v \qquad (A.10)$$

The same kind of argument made in respect to equations (A.2–A.4) holds here: That is, with particles whose rest mass is zero, as long as $v = c$, the equation becomes indeterminate and λ may have a value. In all other cases λ becomes infinite, which leads to two interesting postulates:

1. *An infon is a photon whose wavelength has been stretched to infinity.*

   And conversely,
2. *A photon is an infon travelling at the speed of light.*

An infon may therefore be envisaged as a photon which *appears* to have stopped oscillating: At velocities other than c, its wavelength *appears* infinite, its frequency zero. Once an infon is accelerated to the speed of light, it crosses a threshold which allows it to be perceived as having energy. When that does happen, the energy E becomes a function of its frequency ν, ie:

$$E = h\nu \qquad (A.11)$$

Conversely, at velocities other than c, the particle exhibits neither energy nor momentum – yet it could retain at least two information properties – its speed, and its direction. In other words, **at velocities other than c, a quantum of energy becomes converted into a quantum of information (an infon).**

The above suggests the possibility that the universe is filled with infons. Present techniques, however, are not designed to ascertain the presence of such particles because they are travelling at speeds other than c and therefore fail to interact with matter (ie, they possess no momentum). An infon possessing information which made it equivalent to green light, would not become "visible" as green light until it achieved a velocity of c. Just as the human eye does not perceive electromagnetic radiation below a certain frequency and therefore failed to detect infra-red light until we had the proper techniques to do so, so have we not perceived massless particles at speeds slower than light.

May infons achieve a velocity exceeding c? Equation (A.1) is not much help. If v exceeds c, one ends up with the square root of a negative number, and E becomes equal to a zero divided by an imaginary number – a quantity which has no meaning for us. However, that does not exclude the possibility: Phase waves, as discussed above, may exceed the speed of light and certainly constitute a form of information; and the term $\sqrt{-1}$ is not unknown in quantum mechanics (Schrödinger's operator). In addition, some years ago several searches were made for certain hypothetical particles called "tachyons", particles whose velocity exceeded that of the velocity of light. The argument was put forth (Clay and Crouch 1974) that to obtain a real value for the energy of a particle whose velocity exceeds c, we must suppose that the particle possesses a rest mass m_0 which is not a real number. Instead,

$$m_0 = \mathrm{i}\, m_1 \quad \text{with } m_1 \text{ as real.} \qquad \text{(A.12)}$$

If this extension to theory were valid, then tachyons could exist and their total energy would be given by

$$E = m_1 c_2 \,/\, \sqrt{(v^2/c^2 - 1)} \qquad \text{(A.13)}$$

It follows from this equation that tachyons would exist only at velocities exceeding c, and that their energy would diminish as v increases. The converse of that statement is that a loss of energy would produce an acceleration, which means that a tachyon would have to radiate energy and suffer continuous acceleration. It could not possess uniform motion in a straight line.

Such a charged tachyon was considered to fulfil the conditions for emission of Cerenkov radiation, even in free space.

Of particular interest is the evidence obtained by Clay and Crouch (1974) for the appearance of non-random events preceding the arrival of an extensive cosmic air shower. That is, the first interaction of a primary cosmic-ray nucleon occurs at a typical altitude of 20 km. Further interactions result in a cascade of relativistic particles travelling at velocities close to c. Most of these particles arrive at sea level within a few nanoseconds, creating an extensive air shower (EAS). If any particles are produced during the first interaction (20 km up) which travel faster than c they should be observable at sea level up to 60 μs prior to the EAS. Non-random activity was indeed detected by these workers prior to extensive air showers, suggesting the existence of particles travelling at velocities exceeding *c*.

The idea of tachyons should not be confused with the idea of infons. Tachyons have imaginary mass, ie, m^2 would be a negative value. Infons would possess neither mass nor energy. Nevertheless, the experimental observations cited above, ie, the detection of a secondary event at some distance from the primary event, suggest that the transfer of particles (information?) may occur with a speed exceeding that of light.

The fact that quanta of information (infons) acquire exotic properties (ν, λ, p) when they impinge at speed *c* implies some, as yet unknown, organisational (information) property of the receptors (atoms, pigment molecules, antennae) without which electro-magnetic radiation cannot be detected. Such an interpretation would explain two phenomena: First, irrespective of energy content, the speed of light appears to be constant. Second, no matter at what velocity an observer is travelling relative to a source of radiation, the observer would be able to observe only those quanta travelling at a speed of *c* relative to the observer/detector. Therefore the speed of light would always appear constant.

The most logical way to explain the possibility that only quanta travelling at velocity *c* are perceived by receptors is by invoking that most important of information phenomena: *resonance*. That is, because moving quanta exhibit a double set of oscillations (ie, electric/magnetic and energy/information), successful reception (absorption) must fulfil not only the well-known requirement for *frequency*, but for *velocity* as well. The receptor must be attuned to the entrance velocity of the incoming particle, as well as its alternating electromagnetic fields in order to capture it.

The matter is analogous to attempting to jump into a pair of rotating skipping ropes. Children well versed in the art of skipping ropes know that they must not only jump up and down at an appropriate rate – the *resonance frequency* – but to get in, they must move into the ropes at just the right speed – the correct *entrance velocity*.

Might Atoms Contain Infons?

Let us return to the sign on Times Square. The letters and symbols moving across the field of lighted bulbs are dark. That is, each letter is created by a pattern of electric bulbs which are "off". These "off" states appear as dark "holes" moving across the brightly lit field. Each binary light bulb, therefore, represents not only a discrete *particle* of information but the information is conveyed to the passer-by by means of *holes*.

Holes, or empty spaces, when enclosed in an organised structure may be highly significant pieces of information. For example, the most commonly used symbol in the written English language is the space between words. On a typewriter, the space bar is used more frequently than any other single key. The information content of the space (the hole) between two words disappears the moment the words disappear and one is left with just a blank page. Nevertheless, spaces between organised structures are highly significant because they constitute *boundaries*. Spaces represent discontinuities which define the *limits* of structural entities. This is as true for indicating where a word ends, as for defining a discontinuity in a force field.

Thus we must recognise as axiomatic the statement that: *The absence of structure within a structure, may carry information as real as the structure itself.* Holes and spaces within an organised structure, may comprise a significant part of the organisation of that structure, hence contain information. However, the information content of such holes or spaces is entirely dependent upon the organisation and behaviour of the structures or systems which surround them.

Atomic shells are highly structured entities. If they were not, neither Balmer's ladder, nor Pauli's exclusion principle, nor any number of other atomic phenomena would manifest themselves. When a photon is absorbed by an atom, its *energy* manifests itself by ejecting an electron from an inner shell. At least part (and perhaps all) of the photon's *information* may manifest itself as the hole left in the inner shell which lost the electron. That is, it would not be unreasonable to postulate that:

the hole left in an atomic shell by a lost electron, constitutes a particulate form of information, ie, an infon.

Such holes are known to move across crystalline structures in collective excitations with a velocity, frequency and wave-length. In themselves, they possess neither mass nor momentum, and their velocity is not confined to c. As such, they would fulfil all the requirements of "infons" postulated above.

To *fermions* and *bosons*, therefore, we need to add a third class of particles – *infons*. The first two represent the particulate manifestation of *matter* and *energy*. Infons represent the particulate manifestation of *information*; they include particles such as phonons, excitons, and the holes left in atomic shells by ejected electrons.

Holes comprising particulate information inside organised structures need not be confined only to structures of matter such as a crystal. Such holes may exist inside fields of organised energy such as a gravity field or a magnetic field. Furthermore, there is no reason to believe that such holes could not migrate across such fields as they do across material structures. In other words, infons could move not only inside matter, but across force fields, as well.

How many different kinds of infons actually exist remains to be seen. What is likely, however, is that just as photons are part of the electro-magnetic spectrum comprising a spectrum of *energy*, so may infons comprise a spectrum of *information*.

Literature Cited

RW Clay and PC Crouch (1974) Possible observations of tachyons associated with extensive air showers, *Nature* 248: 28–30.

W Poundstone (1985) *The Recursive Universe*, Contemporary Books, Chicago.

· *Appendix B* ·

Further Speculations : Implications for Atomic Structure

On the Information Content of Intra-atomic Space

Intra-atomic space may be defined as the extra-nuclear space between an atomic nucleus and the outermost potential orbit of its electronic shells. Intra-atomic space represents an information-rich system. It is *not* some vague grey emptiness filled with a thin soup of the statistical probabilities of orbiting electrons. Intra-*atomic* space must be highly organised – as highly organised as intra-*nuclear* space: Even an atom as simple as hydrogen, with its single orbiting electron, must possess an intricately organised intra-atomic space if we are to explain Balmer's ladder, and the fact that the electron appears to be able to move in only a few, select orbits.

The organisation of this intra-atomic space is not dependent primarily on the presence of *matter*. For although orbiting electrons may traverse this space, its structure is largely a reflection of organised *energy*. Organised space may be envisaged as an empty space – space devoid of matter – in which there exists, however, a force-field such as a powerful magnetic field. Such space, which would *appear* empty (and therefore apparently lacking in organisation) in fact, would contain information and organisation. To prove this, one would need only to propel a charged particle through this space, to discover that its path would be altered. That is, the information properties of this organised space, would cause a charged particle to alter both its speed and its direction. To a charged particle, such space would appear curved. In a similar fashion, electric or gravitational fields would cause empty space to be organised. Space, therefore may be organised either by the presence of patterns of matter, or patterns of energy.

Intra-atomic space, subjected to electric, magnetic, and other force fields as well as the organised distribution of matter, must

perforce, have a highly differentiated structure – a "*morphe*".*
That morphe reflects the specific organisation of the fermions, bosons, and infons comprising the atom. Among the extra-nuclear bosons are the photons. If the earlier speculations prove correct this space would also contain infons. Most important, this space and its component fermions (electrons), bosons, and infons cannot be static. It would be unstable. Stability would be achieved by a dynamic, spinning or orbiting system with feedback mechanisms which result in resonances. These resonances, in turn, produce regular oscillations. The atom, in other words, pulses at fixed frequencies.

Each kind of atom has a unique morphe characterising its intra-atomic space. This uniqueness is utilised when applying nuclear magnetic resonance (NMR) techniques for studying matter. NMR reflects the composition of the nucleus and its spin. The magnetic field surrounding a spinning nucleus is but one of many forces which define and differentiate the morphe of intra-atomic space. Electron spin is another.

In the light of all that has been said previously, it would not seem unreasonable to postulate that when holes (infons) are created in the inner shells of atoms by the photo-induced ejection of electrons into outer shells, such holes continue to orbit the nucleus. In fact, one could readily envisage that the space surrounding the nucleus is filled with numerous orbiting holes which form a pattern (for example, as hollow shells). Furthermore, this pattern of orbiting holes in the extra-nuclear space, together with the pattern of orbiting electrons and rotating forces, provides each atom with a clearly defined morphe.

---

* The introduction of the term "morphe" is to get away from the term "structure". "Structure" has the connotation of the structure of a building, a crystal, or an atomic nucleus. "Structure" conveys an imagery of solid blocks of matter joined to form a structure. Insofar as the intra-atomic space external to the nucleus also has a structure, but one based not on matter but largely on interacting force fields, it is probably helpful to utilize another term. "Morphe" is derived from the Greek work for form (morphe). Like the word "psyche" (derived from psukhe), denoting the totality of the spirit of an object or person, the morphe of a system should denote its totality of form – that is, the organisation of matter, energy, and information. The study of atomic "morphes" would be atomic "morphology", a branch of physics which would concern itself not only with the structure of the nucleus, but with the extra-nuclear space as well. Atomic morphology would be crucial to the chemist and crystallographer since the extra-nuclear morphe of an atom would determine its chemical behaviour, or how atoms line up in a crystal.

If holes can orbit a nucleus, there is no reason to assume that they might not be able to escape. On the basis of previous considerations one could conceive of at least two quite distinct mechanisms: The first is illustrated by putting a sufficiently strong electric charge across a semiconductor material forcing electrons to migrate, and the holes to apparently migrate in the opposite direction. In this case the infons retain their integrity as migrating holes. In the second case, an electron orbiting in an outer shell, drops down into an inner shell. The energy released by this reorganisation, somehow combines with the hole left behind in the outer shell, to create a photon. This photon, ie, this energised infon, now migrates outward with speed c and escapes into the surrounding medium of force fields.

In both instances, the migrating packets of information are propelled by an input of energy. That is, just as it takes energy to propel a body of matter, so does it take energy to propel a body of information. Unlike the former, however, information particles possess no mass.

If electromagnetic waves involve a *double* set of oscillations, they can migrate across the organised force fields of intra-atomic space only when properly attuned to its resonances. Such attuning requires a constant speed: the light constant *c*. Therefore, intra-atomic space acts as the equivalent of an "ether": It propagates waves of electromagnetic energy just as air propagates sound waves. However, whereas sound waves involve the transmission of energy via a medium consisting of particles of matter (eg, air molecules), the intra-atomic space is filled with a medium of bosons acting as force fields. Just as the speed of sound is dependent on the organisational properties of the transmitting medium, so is the speed of electromagnetic radiation determined by the organisational properties of this intra-atomic space.

Earlier, we alluded to the "Game of Life", a recursive program played on a computer screen. We gave the example of the "Glider" as the example of an oscillating configuration which "glides" across the screen. The *direction* of movement is determined by the information (instructions) provided by the computer program. However, *the rate of propagation* is determined by the rate at which the individual cells turn on and off, which is determined by the *rate* at which the computer is ticking over. In other words, the velocity at which the Glider moves is a function of the rate of oscillation of a recursive system, ie, the time it takes to complete a single cycle. One could envisage a comparable circumstance for the propagation of light across intra-atomic space. This could be the key: Only when the moving quantum propagates at velocity c is it "in tune" with the recursive cycles of the pulsating atom. Only then may it be captured, and only then will it appear to possess momentum – its apparent energy correlating with its frequency (ie, the electric/magnetic alternations).

The major difference between a quantum and a Glider is that the latter is totally dependent on the medium of the screen, whereas a quantum of light may "escape" and move out beyond the boundaries of intra-atomic space. The boundary of the computer screen, the cathode ray tube, is precisely and rigidly delineated. In contrast, at least some of the forces comprising organised intra-atomic space, extend beyond the outermost reaches of the electron shells. Such a lack of rigid boundary conditions may create a gradient which not only makes "escape" possible, but may influence the velocity and properties of incoming quanta. It is conceivable that quanta, whose velocities are not too far removed from c in respect to the intra-atomic space, might be modulated to move at the correct speed. In any case, one could envisage that the propagation of quanta of energy/information at velocities c across intra-atomic space reflects the endogenous oscillations of atoms whose recursive pulsations occur with a periodicity which is some function of c.

Parenthetically, if there does exist a kind of infon which represents the fundamental and universal unit of time – a chronon – it is likely to be based on the time it takes to complete a single cycle of the atomic pulse. Such pulse time would be independent of atomic weight and number, but would be related to the velocity of light. This assertion is based on the observation that the properties of intra-atomic space are such that they vary from one kind of atom to the next as far as the *frequency* of a photon is concerned, but seem to be uniform with respect to the *velocity* of propagation of light quanta. The velocity of light may vary, however, in those interatomic spaces where forces overlap, as inside a molecule, a crystal, or other forms of interacting matter. That is, where matter is sufficiently dense, the velocity of propagation is determined by the information properties of the overlapping atomic fields comprising the propagating medium.

If we postulate that light cannot traverse the intra-atomic medium at any speed other than c, then it would not be unreasonable to postulate that quanta *leaving* the intra-atomic space, do so at an initial velocity *c* with respect to the emitting atom. Unless they become subjected to other forces, their velocity would remain at *c* in respect to their source as they traversed outer space.

Conversely, quanta from some external source entering intra-atomic space, can be propagated inside atomic space *only* if they travel at speed *c* with respect to the absorbing atom. Depending on their energy or other resonance properties, eg, "frequency", the incoming photon (moving at *c*) may now interact with its host atom in one of several ways: The photon may be absorbed by the atom. This process, as discussed above, is accompanied by a change in the information state of the extra-nuclear, atomic space: An electron is bounced out into a thermodynamically more improbable outer shell. The energy of the absorbed photon has been converted into an increase in the information content of the atom. The atom has acquired additional *structural* information if the new arrangement is stable – *kinetic* information if the electron drops back down emitting a photon of less energy. The differences in wavelength of absorbed and emitted light, the increase in entropy, represent the "cost" of all that information processing.

The concept of organised intra-atomic space as postulated above – ie, of an extra-nuclear morphe – would allow an alternative interpretation of the Compton effect. The incoming photon, responsible for ejecting the electron, is causing a reorganisation of this morphe. Insofar as the outgoing photon can traverse the intra-atomic space only at velocity *c*, its escape velocity, likewise will be *c*. This accounts for the observation that the velocity of the photons before and after "collision" does not change, only that there is an increase in wavelength. *Information physics would view the photoelectric effect*, and its inverse, X-ray production, not in terms of a collision of particles, *but as a form of instantaneous information processing* by the resonances of organised intra-atomic space, keeping in mind that a change in information status may express itself as a change in energy status.

Finally, in considering the propagation of blobs of the "escaped resonances" (quanta) across the universe, once the idea of organised space is accepted, it follows naturally that there may exist a propagating medium even though such a medium is devoid of matter. In deep space, the most likely candidate for organising space is gravity. However, gravity fields vary in density and distribution, and must interact with other forces. Thus the velocity of quanta may vary. As stated above, in order for such quanta to exhibit relativistic momentum, and therefore be perceived, such quanta must be modulated to travel at velocity c in respect to the receptor – keeping in mind, that all known receptors consist of atoms or combinations of atoms.

If a force such as gravity is, in fact, responsible for the organisational properties of space which allow for the propagation of quanta, then a Michelson–Morley type experiment is foredoomed to failure. At the surface of the earth, the bulk of the gravity originates from the earth itself, and moves with the earth. To an observer on the earth's surface the gravity field would appear stationary and therefore would not fulfil the requirement for the concept of a moving earth travelling through a stationary ether. The overlapping gravitational fields emanating from the moon, the sun, and the planets fluctuate too slowly to affect the experiment observably. Only a rapid pulse of a significant gravity wave would affect the measurement of light.

Interstellar gravitational waves are, in fact, thought to exist – the strongest emanating from objects such as stellar binaries and type II supernovas. A series of gravitational wave observatories are planned for the 1990s in Europe and North America (see Jeffries et al. 1987). It is interesting to note that the experimental set-up in these observatories involves laser interferometers – measuring two light paths at right angles to each other – in principle a Michelson–Morley type experiment. However, if a gravitational wave is detected in such a system, the resulting wave shift is to be interpreted in terms of the gravitational distortion of the interferometer – the relative movement of the two mirrors with respect to each other – rather than as any direct effect on the speed/wavelength of the light in the two arms of the interferometer. Perhaps another experiment could be added to see if a strong gravity wave causes a shift in the velocity of light.

Literature Cited

AD Jeffries, PR Saulson, RE Spero and ME Zucker (1987) Gravitational wave observatories, *Sci. Am.* 256(6):50–60.

· *Appendix C* ·

A Smaller Universe?

If the analysis presented thus far, concerning the existence and velocities of infons, proves to be correct, then there could be implications for judging the distances of stars.

At present, astronomers associate a red shift with receding stellar objects. As stated so clearly over 50 years ago by Edwin Hubble (1936), in general, fainter nebulae, needing more powerful telescopes to be observed, are associated with a greater shift towards the red. The explanation consistent with these observations assumes an expanding universe in which the galaxies which are the farthest from us appear to be moving away at the greatest speed. The faintest galaxies are accelerating away from us the fastest, and the faintest are assumed to be the farthest away.

This last correlation may need to be reconsidered, if one is prepared to accept that whereas quanta of light can be propagated only at velocity c, quanta of information (infons) may be propagated at any speed.

Consider a star receding from us at velocity v. Assume that the emission of electromagnetic radiation can only involve an initial (ejecting) velocity of c. However, if infons do exist, the emitted quanta of light can be readily transformed into quanta of pure information which may travel at any velocity. Such quanta, therefore, would impinge on earth with a velocity of $(c-v)$. They would not possess the properties of quanta of light, but rather act as quanta of information – lacking momentum, frequency and wavelength. Therefore, at velocity $(c-v)$, such particles would not be detected by earthly receptors.

In order for quanta to be perceived, they must impinge on

earthly receptors at velocity c, not $(c-v)$. The only way this is possible is if some of the quanta approaching earth were accelerated.

If gravity does prove to be involved with the propagating of quanta, one could postulate that the stronger the gravity field, the greater the *velocity* of the quanta. That is, the velocity of quanta traversing space as infons, is determined by the *strength* of the gravitational field acting as the propagating medium. This would account for the apparent curvature of space around bodies with gravitational fields. A gravitational field, if it causes an apparent curvature in time/space, must represent an organisational property of the system. Gravity therefore, has a substantial information component – it could, in fact, be envisaged as exerting its "force" by virtue of the information it confers on time/space structures. If this is true, one would expect infons approaching the earth's gravitational field to be accelerated.

Of all the quanta emitted by the star receding with a velocity v, only those accelerated to a velocity $(c + v)$ would impinge on earthly receptors at velocity c, and would be converted to, and therefore be detectable as, light quanta coming from that star.

If this is true, then one would expect two features to be associated with such a process. The first is a red shift. If the frequency of the quantum is an unchanging, intrinsic information property conferred by the resonance structure of the emitter, then at constant frequency any increase in velocity would automatically cause an increase in wavelength.

Second, other things being equal, the greater the velocity at which the star is receding, the smaller will be the fraction of quanta which will have acquired the extra compensatory velocity $(c + v)$ to arrive at earth with velocity c. That is, if we assume a statistical distribution of velocities of the emitted quanta as they approach earth, with the bulk being propagated at, or near, velocity c (in respect to the emitting star), then the further from the norm, the smaller the fraction of the incoming quanta which can be "seen". Actually, the norm may be displaced from c by various forces encountered during the journey across space. Nevertheless, if we assume two equally luminescent stars, equidistant from earth (at time zero), if one of the two is receding at a greater velocity, it will appear fainter because only a smaller fraction of its emission will be "seen" by us.

Thus the correlation of red shift with faintness of light could result from the velocity with which a star is receding, rather than merely reflecting its distance from the observer. If this is true, the faintest stars with the greatest red shift may not be as far from us as presently calculated.

Invisible Stars?

A red shift would involve the acceleration of infons to velocity *c* at which state they would become detectable as photons. A blue shift would involve the opposite mechanism – a slowing down of photons to achieve velocity *c*. Since the earth's gravity would tend to accelerate incoming infons, one would expect to "see" a far greater proportion of cosmic objects exhibiting red shifts than blue shifts.

It should be emphasised that the velocity–distance relationship, given the state of our present knowledge, is nowhere as clear-cut as is usually implied. For example, L. Parish (1981) has pointed out that [p. 6] "the only proven fact about the cosmological red-shifts is that they are observable" – the rest is conjecture. Parish's criticism has force insofar as he lists the considerable discrepancies (up to an order of magnitude) in Hubble constants calculated by various prominent astronomers [table 3, p. 40]. Parish himself ascribes the bulk of the red shifts to the transverse movement of the solar system within our galaxy (250 km/s).

Parish, and other authors, have also questioned the lack of observable blue-shift phenomena: "One would expect blue-shifts to be observable looking forward (along the rotation) along the tangent of the disc of the Galaxy, just as red-shifts might be expected looking backwards" [pp. 26–27]. If the infon theory proves correct, one would not expect to see a star or galaxy which is moving towards us at a significant speed. Here the bulk of quanta impinging on earth would possess a velocity of $(c + v)$. Unless such quanta, while traversing space, were significantly slowed down, an observer on earth would detect no electromagnetic radiation whatsoever. It may turn out that when, in the 1990s, the system of gravity detectors is in place, we will observe sources of gravity implying the presence of a mass, yet detect no electromagnetic radiation. This could be either a black hole, or represent a body moving towards us.

Recently, astronomers have established the presence of brown and black dwarf stars in the galactic environs of the sun. Some of these appear to be quite close to the solar system, causing unexplained perturbations in the orbits of the comets. One possible explanation centres on the suggestion that a black dwarf star is approaching the sun fairly rapidly. Another set of theories considers that the sun has a twin – a dwarf red star called Nemesis with which it interacts periodically and whose gravitational effects cause major geological disturbances on earth (resulting in the extinction of large classes of fauna). The periodicity of Nemesis is thought to be approximately 30 million years.

If, indeed, such a star were approaching us at a significant speed, the infon theory would predict that it would be nearly invisible. It would also provide a means of testing the infon theory:

Assuming that a star approaches us at velocity v, then as discussed above, the infons would be approaching earth with a velocity of $(c + v)$, therefore would be invisible. The pull of earth's gravity would accelerate these particles still further, and only an occasional particle would be slowed down sufficiently to be perceived at the earth's surface. On the other hand, infons travelling through the earth would be subjected to all the force fields characteristic of space densely packed with matter. Like photons passing through matter (but perhaps involving a different mechanism), infons would be slowed down. Some of them would tend to stabilise at velocity c, therefore could be seen. For this reason, it would become possible to detect electromagnetic radiation emitted by an approaching (apparently) black star only underground. It would become a problem analogous to looking for neutrinos.

The problem arises that if the detector is not sufficiently far underground, the infons might not be slowed enough to achieve velocity c, therefore would remain invisible. On the other hand, once the infons *are* slowed to velocity c, they would behave as any electromagnetic radiation and become promptly absorbed by matter. Therefore, the depth of the detectors would be critical. Alternatively, interposing a transparent or translucent layer of material such as air, glass, or water, might greatly improve the chances of detecting infons becoming converted to photons. Unfortunately there exists no information on the rate of deceleration of infons passing through various kinds of matter, or for that matter, passing through electric, magnetic or gravitational fields.

If it were possible to create a system which could act as an *infon detector*, among the first targets to be re-examined should be the Bok globules. These small, dark objects, named in honour of the Dutch astronomer Bart J. Bok, are thought to represent protostars not yet hot enough to shine (Moore 1986). However, it might turn out that some of these globules are actually stellar objects moving towards us – their blackness caused not by the very low intensity of their electromagnetic radiation emitted, but because the radiation reaches us at velocities exceeding *c*.

Needless to say, should it become possible, by the use of appropriate filtering techniques, to make visible black objects approaching our solar system, then such an observation would provide strong evidence for the existence of quanta of information (infons) being propagated through space at velocities exceeding *c*, and for their inconvertibility into quanta of light (photons) once their velocity has been slowed to *c*.

Literature Cited

E Hubble (1936) *The Realm of the Nebulae*, Oxford University Press, London.
P Moore (1986) *A–Z of Astronomy*, Patrick Stephens, Wellingborough.
L Parish (1981) *The Theory of Cosmic Aberration*, Cortney Publications, Luton.

· *Appendix D* ·

Other Universes?

Traditional physics has tried to cram a three-parameter universe into a two-parameter system of explanation. It has overlooked the hidden dimension. Matter and energy comprise merely the surface – the internal structure of the universe contains information.

We know that matter and energy are interconvertible. We accept, however, a great divide. It is problematic to explain motion solely in terms of matter. It is inconvenient to explain mass solely in terms of energy. So we analyse the phenomena encountered in the universe in terms of various forms of matter and energy. We appear to be loath, however, to accord equal importance to distance, time, and direction. Although we can measure and define them with precision, they cannot be explained either in terms of energy, or of matter.

Distance, time and direction are inherently tied to velocity, acceleration, force, and work. These quantities, therefore, cannot be considered merely as a function of energy. None of these make sense in the absence of a frame of reference – a bit of the universe that is organised. "Information" is as vital to the analysis of motion as is "energy". This is as true for the internal motion of a particle (spin) as it is for its external motion. Similarly, to consider a positive charge to be the inherent property of protons, and charm or beauty to be an inherent property of quarks, is like considering heat to be an inherent property of metals. It can be done. But it is shirking the in-depth analysis which needs to be made.

In line with these considerations, let us now represent the structure of the universe in terms of *three* axes consisting of matter m, energy e, and information i (see fig. D.1).

Each axis corresponds to pure matter m, or energy e, or information i. The m axis, lacking both information and energy would consist of randomly distributed, unlinked fundamental particles at 0 K. The e axis would consist of pure energy in an infinite entropy state. The i axis containing neither matter, nor energy would consist of infons propagating through empty space. The origin would be represented by absolutely empty space, at absolute zero, devoid of all information. Presumably these states do not exist in nature.

The three planes created by two of the three components would provide the theoretical boundaries of our present universe. The (m,i) plane would contain zero energy. The temperature in this plane would be absolute zero (0 K). The (m,i) plane would contain both matter and information. The matter would be organised into perfect crystals. Under such conditions it would be possible to measure distances, but perhaps not time. In the absence of any motion, or events, time might be frozen.

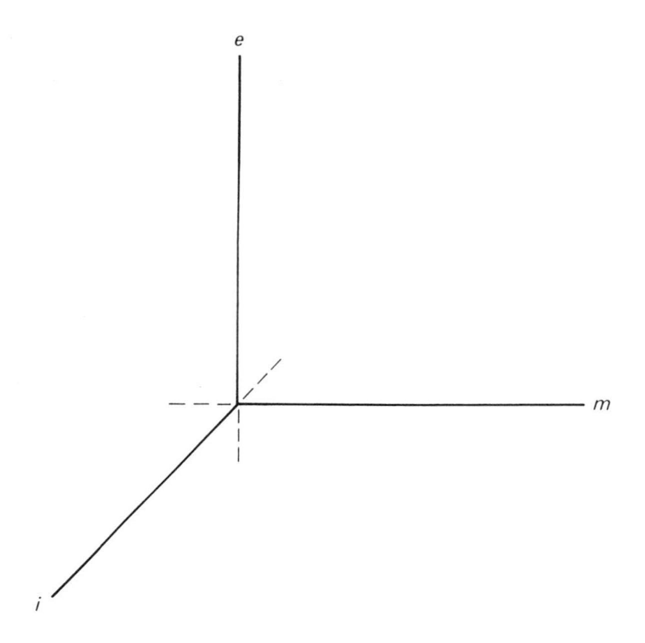

Figure D.1

The (e,i) plane would contain zero matter. It would contain both energy and information. The (e,i) plane would therefore consist of an absolute vacuum traversed by force fields and pulses of energy. Under such circumstances it would be possible to measure time but perhaps not distances. Inside an absolute vacuum there are no material landmarks. Empty space may be impossible to measure without introducing a frame of reference, and therefore distance may have no meaning.

The (m,e) plane would contain zero information. It would contain both matter and energy. The matter would contain no structural information, therefore consist only of fundamental particles. The energy would consist only of heat, and therefore would possess no kinetic information. In other words, the (m,e) plane would consist of fundamental particles moving at random – neither the particles nor the entire mass exhibiting any organisation whatsoever. Under such conditions there would be no landmarks and no events. Therefore, it would become impossible to measure either time or space, and therefore these forms of information would not exist.

The three planes described above – (m,e), (m,i), (e,i) would represent the theoretical limits of phenomena observable in our ordinary world. The negative energy state implied by the Dirac equations, followed by the subsequent demonstration of the existence of anti-matter, however, implies that both the e and the m axes may possess negative values, going beyond the origin into a negative realm. If that is so, might there not exist worlds with anti-information, as well? Should that prove to be true, then ours is but one of eight possible universes. To move into any of the others, one would need to traverse certain barriers – an absolute vacuum to arrive at the anti-matter universe, the absolute zero temperature state to enter the anti-energy universe, and the zero information (infinite entropy) state to observe the anti-information universe.

The idea of an absolute vacuum, or of absolute zero temperature have been around for a long time. In traditional physics, the idea of a zero information state, however, has never been clearly envisaged. Earlier in this book, it was equated to an infinite entropy state. From the point of view of information physics, a good candidate for a zero information state is the centre of a black hole. Clearly, a black hole is rich in matter and energy. However, the enormous pressures may cause matter to be reduced to its most elementary particles, while inside the collapsing black hole, the energy created and absorbed is randomly distributed. Thus while a black hole in this universe is a highly differentiated event with a defined location – therefore the hole as a whole posesses information – *inside* the black hole, there may exist a zero information state.

If the inside of a black hole does contain a zero information state, then such a region may represent the interface with a negative information universe.

What would be the attributes of a negative information universe? Depending on which quadrant, the equations describing our laws of physics would have to be recast. In some instances, positive entities would become negative, variables appearing in the numerator might appear in the denominator (and vice versa), the entropy associated with most energetic reactions might actually decrease, while time might run backwards. This last possibility is not wholly outlandish in the light of Richard Feynman's demonstration that mathematically, a positron may be regarded as an electron moving backward in time.

The eight universes implied in fig. D.1 are more likely to represent eight states of a single universe. Therefore, although one may speak of eight universes, it should be viewed as a literary device for differentiating the eight states.

If the "big bang" theory of the origin of the universe is correct, one could envisage two things: First, that the big bang itself represented a shift of the universe from one state to another – a shift which might be described with precision by utilising the mathematics of catastrophe theory. Second, that the sequence of events following the big bang provides a clue as to where (which alternate state) our present universe came from. After the big bang the following evolutionary steps (as reviewed by Burns 1986): At t_0, zero information – the point universe is in a totally undifferentiated state – even the four known fundamental forces are unformed. After 10^{-43} seconds, gravity differentiates out from the other three forces, which remain unified until after 10^{-35} seconds, at which time the strong nuclear force differentiates from the electroweak force. This results in a rapid expansion, the universe becoming a hot soup of quarks and electrons. As the universe achieves the ripe old age of one second, nucleosynthesis begins as quarks bind together to form protons, while the electromagnetic and weak forces differentiate. During the next 100,000 years (10^{12}

seconds), protons and electrons join to form neutrons, which, in turn, combine with other protons to form the atomic nuclei of deuterium, helium, and lithium. Matter then decouples from radiation and the universe becomes transparent. Radiation now streams freely through space. In due course, the further evolution of matter into various elements – the condensation of matter into discrete bodies – the cooling of the earth and the formation of crystals – and after many billions of years the appearance of life.

If the concept of an eight-state universe is correct, then, judging from the sequence of events, the big bang creating our contemporary universe would represent a crossing via the *e* axis. That is, the progenitor of our present state consisted of an anti-matter, negative information (but positive energy) universe.

Following the big bang, the primordial system was losing energy. However, while energy was being lost, matter as we know it, was being created. Part of that process involved an increase in organisation: For example, from quarks to nucleons to atoms. Thus energy was being converted not only into matter, but into structural information as well.

This is one of the key insights of information physics: While the energy of the universe appears to be dissipating towards its ultimate state – the entropic death – there also exist processes which convert energy into information. Thus there exist two mutually contradictory forces: The first leads to an increase in entropy, the second to an increase in information. The latter of these processes has evolved into a new phenomenon – *Intelligence* – which supersedes information. It is a recent phenomenon and its impact on the evolution of the universe remains to be seen. It cannot be ignored.

Barrow and Tipler (1986) in their book The *Anthropic Cosmological Principle* have reviewed the evolution of thinking among scientists concerned with the evolution of the universe. They define the weak anthropic principle [p. 16] as follows: "The observed values of all physical and cosmological quantities are not equally probable but they take on values restricted by the requirements that there exist sites where carbon-based life can evolve and by the requirement that the Universe be old enough for it to have already done so." The authors develop their theme to its logical conclusion [pp. 676–677] viz, in due course, life will engulf the entire universe and approach the

"Omega Point". At the instant the Omega Point is reached, life will "have stored an infinite amount of information, including all bits of knowledge which it is logically possible to know. And this is the end."

If the eight-state model of the universe actually does exist, Barrow and Tipler's Omega Point would be equivalent to the i axis, and would presage a transition of our present universe into an anti-matter, anti-energy (but positive information) state.

Alternatively, if the "entropic death" scenario were to prevail, a random dispersal of matter, a few degrees above 0 K, would imply a position in the (e,m) plane near the m axis. Once it broke through that barrier, the universe would end up in a negative information (but positive matter and energy) state.

Our universe began as pure energy. Irrespective of whether it ends up organised as pure information, or as a lethargic, disorganised entropic soup, the idea of an eight-state universe implies a pulsating, oscillating system.

Literature Cited

JD Barrow and FJ Tipler (1986) *The Anthropic Cosmological Principle*, Clarendon Press, Oxford.

JO Burns (1986) Very large structures in the universe, *Sci. Am.* 255(1):30–39.

Subject Index